They Dance in the Sky

Native American Star Myths

They Dance in the Sky

Native American Star Myths

Jean Guard Monroe
and
Ray A. Williamson

Illustrations by Edgar Stewart

Houghton Mifflin Company
Boston

ACKNOWLEDGMENTS

Numerous individuals have assisted us in various ways to complete this book. We wish to thank especially those who took time out of their busy schedules to read and comment on it in draft. Von Del Chamberlain, Claire R. Farrer, and M. Jane Young helped us ensure the accuracy of the explanatory material. Any errors that may have crept in, however, remain our responsibility alone. Dennis Brezina, Karen Caruso, Christy Fiedler, Barbara Lee, and Ebby Malmgren read and commented on early versions of several stories. Carol Carnett, Gregory Mestanas, Tanya Taylor, and Barbara Vaughan provided us with many constructive suggestions about improving the book's readability.

We thank the Smithsonian Institution Anthropological Archives and the Holland Library of Washington State University for their assistance in obtaining original notes and manuscripts. Karen Lupardas provided useful linguistic information about the Alabama Indians.

Finally, we wish to thank Matilda Welter, our editor at Houghton Mifflin, for her constructive editorial suggestions, as well as all the others who made publication of this book possible.

Printed in the United States of America **HAL** 10 9 8 7 6

Library of Congress Cataloging-in-Publication Data

Monroe, Jean.
They dance in the sky.

Includes bibliographies and index.
Summary: A collection of legends about the stars from various North American Indian cultures, including explanations of the Milky Way and constellations such as the Big Dipper.
1. Indians of North America—Legends. 2. Indians of North America—Religion and mythology—Juvenile literature. 3. Stars—Folklore—Juvenile literature. [1. Indians of North America—Legends. 2. Stars—Folklore] I. Williamson, Ray A., 1938– II. Title.
E98.F6M66 1987 398.2'6 86-27547
ISBN 0-395-39970-X

To our children — Jeffrey, Michael, Brian, and Stephanie — Ethan and Sarah — whose questions showed the necessity for such a book and whose interest helped keep it going.

Song of the Stars

We are the Stars which sing,
We sing with our light.
We are the birds of fire,
We fly over the sky.
Our light is a voice,
We make a road
For the spirit to pass over.

— ALGONQUIN SONG

Contents

	Preface	ix
1	Seven Dancing Stars: *Legends of the Pleiades*	1
2	The Celestial Bear: *Stories of the Big Dipper*	15
3	Coyote Scatters the Stars: *Myths from the Southwest*	28
4	When Stars Fell to Earth: *Legends of the Pawnee*	44
5	Morning Star: *Legends of the Plains Indians*	63
6	They Live in the Sky: *Stories of the California Indians*	79
7	Chinook Wind: *Stories from the Northwest Coast*	95
8	Star Beings: *Tales from the Southeast*	107
	Glossary	119
	Suggested Further Reading	124
	Bibliography	125
	Index	128

Preface

American Indian folklore and mythology are rich in tales of the natural world and how humans relate to it. Sky stories play an especially important part in these accounts of the world. Many of them tell about the Beginning Time, when animals could speak and people could change into animal shapes and back with ease. At that time, the earth was young and pliable, and monsters often roamed at will. Human beings were lifted into the sky, and sky beings came to earth.

During the last years of the nineteenth century and the first decades of the twentieth, these myths and tales were collected by scholars and others who recognized their beauty and their importance in describing the Native American view of the world. They wished to save them for others to enjoy before Anglo-European culture buried them forever.

Native Americans had no written language, so they transmitted their ideas orally. (Most tribes still do not write in their own language, depending instead on English or Spanish.) The master storytellers, both men and women, learned the legends from their elders and sometimes embellished them as they passed them on to the next generation. Though many of the smaller tribes have virtually disappeared, the storytelling tradition is very much alive today.

How are we to understand these myths? Certainly not as "just-so" stories about the way things were, or as scientific explanations of the natural world. They are allegories or parables that attempt to explain what it means to be human in an often unfriendly world. Some tell how people should act and how to obey the customs of the tribe. Others simply describe the way things are or how they came to be. Some stories are regarded as sacred; others are not. All of them give tribal members standards to live by.

Native Americans who live by traditional beliefs hold that humans are an integral part of nature and should be in harmony with it. And if people want to learn how to live, they must carefully observe the rules and cycles of the natural world.

Most of the stories here have not been published for the general reader before. We found them in scholarly books and in the unpublished notes of scholars. Our hope is to convey some of the excitement of these myths and to put them in the context of the world from which they came, a world that for many tribes is nearly lost.

From the first story about the Pleiades, in which Onondaga children ignore the warnings of an elder, to the last tale, in which a Cherokee dog scatters cornmeal to make the Milky Way, each myth shows a different facet of Native American life and belief. Although many tribes shared some profound similarities, such as the belief that everything in nature was a living being, they also exhibited a tremendous diversity, even before they were influenced by the ideas and customs of European settlers. Because Native Americans lived close to nature and inhabited such varied climatic and geographical settings, the people of one region responded differently to their environment than did those of another. All groups, however, had a deep interest in the stars and their motions throughout the year.

When these tales were told, usually on a winter night with everyone sitting quietly about the fire, the children and adults who listened discussed with the storytellers the meaning of the stories and learned from them. Storytelling is an art, a performance in which a slight change in the speaker's voice, or a simple hand movement, can often say as much as the words themselves. Written down, the stories often lose much of their liveliness and power. We have attempted to make them more accessible without unduly embellishing them. We have clarified the stories where the details are vague in the original. They are meant to be read aloud. It is our hope that, just as the stars retrace their course across the sky, these stories will be read aloud again and again in family groups.

In comparing these stories with myths and tales from other cultures, we see motifs common to many. Themes of order and disorder, curiosity and defiance, love and hate, assume as great a part in Native American thought as they do in the ideas of other peoples around the world. For example, in "The Little Girl Who Scatters the Stars" and in "Coyote Scatters the Stars" we see the same theme of overwhelming curiosity revealed in the Greek myth of Pandora's box. "The Land of the Dead" reminds us of the Greek story of Orpheus and Eurydice. These examples illustrate the universal concern with appropriate behavior that is common to all mythology.

Like storytellers in other countries, Native American storytellers often personify the stars. For example, many cultural groups think of the Pleiades, a tight cluster of stars that grace the winter sky, as dancers. Indeed, as they rise twinkling on crisp winter nights, we can easily imagine that these stars are dancing. The constellation we call the Big Dipper was thought of as a bear or other hunted animal by ancient Greeks and by early European storytellers as well as by many different Native American groups.

In the first two chapters, we have assembled stories about the Pleiades and the Big Dipper because they show how different Native American tribes saw these two well-known and widely recognized stellar patterns. The following chapters present sky stories, including a few more about the Pleiades and the Big Dipper, in a regional context, to give a better understanding of the cultures from which these myths and tales derive. Where possible, we have identified the more familiar constellation names from the Western tradition, so you can find them on a star map. In some cases we could not match Native American constellations with them, either because the available information was too scanty or because Native Americans group the stars differently.

They Dance in the Sky

Native American Star Myths

Pleiades

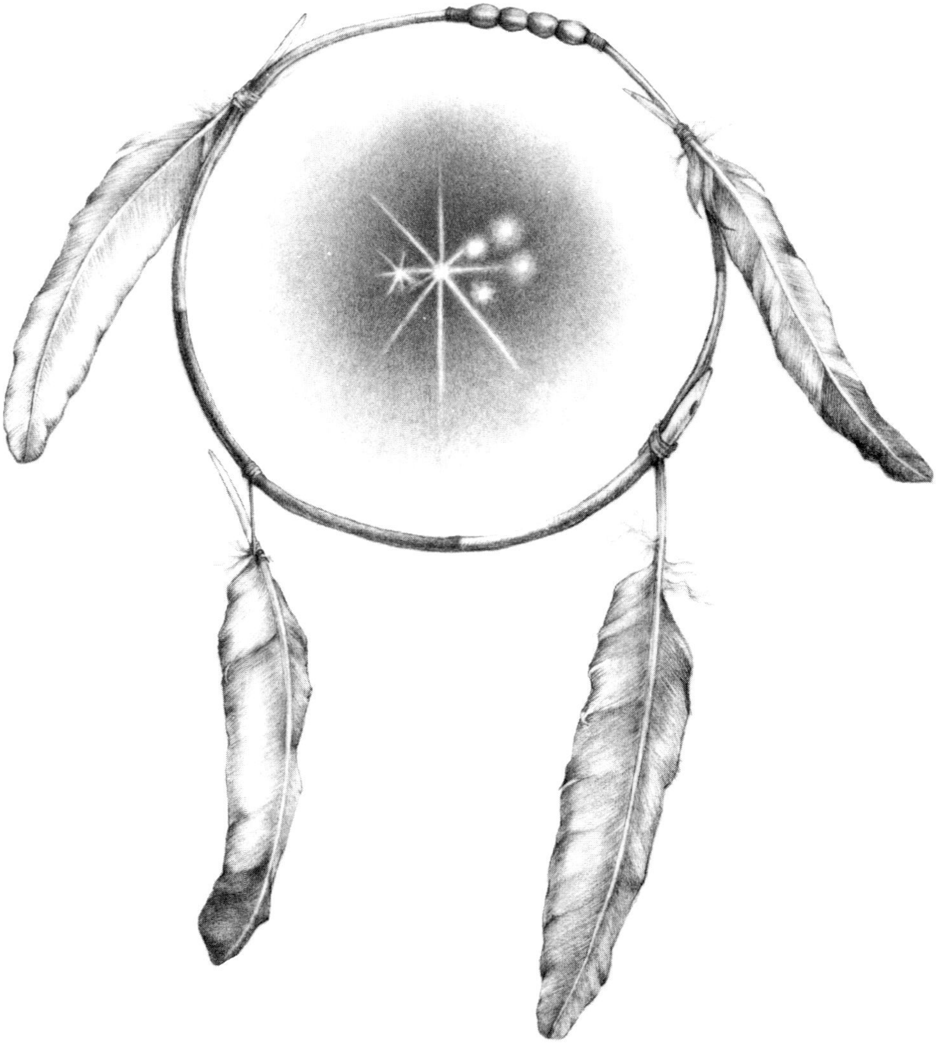

CHAPTER ONE

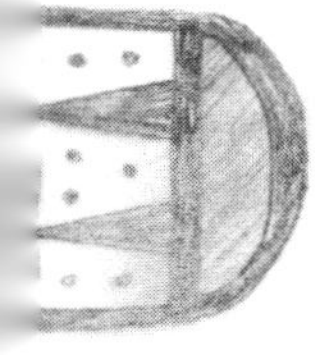

Seven Dancing Stars

Legends of the Pleiades

The small cluster of stars we call the Pleiades is one of the most important constellations of mythology. Nearly every society or people in the world has told stories about the Pleiades. According to one ancient Greek story, they were the Seven Sisters, young daughters of the nymph Pleione. The hunter Orion saw the girls in the forest one day and began to pursue them. They ran from him, appealing for protection to the god Zeus. Zeus took pity on them and turned them into pigeons, who flew to the sky to escape Orion. Though the hunter never caught them, their story lives on in the winter sky. Year after year the constellation Orion continues to pursue the girls, followed by his dog, the bright star Sirius.

The Australian native peoples, the Aborigines, also think of the cluster as young girls. The girls are musicians who play for the Aborigine constellation the Young Men (the three stars of Orion's belt). The Hindus of India saw the Pleiades as the six nurses who cared for one of the sons of the god Siva. They pictured them in the shape of a flame, to honor Agni, the Hindu god of fire.

This compact cluster of stars is honored more than any other stellar pattern because, though relatively faint, it is easily recognizable and because it helps define a calendar. In most parts of the world where it can be seen, the appearance of the Pleiades signals some important event in the year. For example, each year the Tapirapé Indians, who live in the rain forests along the Amazon, watch carefully for the first disappearance of the Pleiades as a sign that the rainy season will soon end. During the rainy season they set the times of certain ceremonies by watching the nightly progression of the Pleiades.

Throughout North America, Native Americans have told stories about this tiny constellation and used it to organize their calendars. Some tribes watched the unique bunch of stars before it disappeared in the sunsets of early spring for clues about when to begin their yearly planting. When the Pleiades reappeared in the early dawns of mid-June, Native American farmers knew that the last of the seeds should be planted immediately or the crops would not mature before autumn's first killing frost. The Pleiades' distinctive shape helped reinforce their calendar message, for among other things the Pleiades reminded the watchers of a heap of seeds and symbolized the hope of plenty in the coming harvest. The Zuni Indians of New Mexico call the Pleiades simply the Seeds, because of their shape and their use in deciding when to plant. Long after planting was over, when the constellation had moved far enough from the sun to appear overhead in the early morning, the astronomer-priests of Zuni and other southwestern pueblos knew that it was time to harvest and that the first frosts were not far behind.

Nor was storytelling time far behind. The Pleiades were a favorite subject of the storytellers, because they were easy to pick out among the other stellar patterns. They were also visible all night during the winter, when everyone would settle down in the early evening to hear the wonderful stories of the First Days, or the ridiculous but instructive tales of Coyote.

Dancing appears time and again as a theme in the stories. Indeed, the seven stars look a bit like two rows of dancers moving gracefully across the sky. Dancing formed an important part of Native American ritual and was connected with fertility and propagation of crops. The people thought of dance itself as a sort of prayer.

Another important theme was the punishment of wrongdoing. Sometimes it was a matter of simple disobedience. At other times, the offense was more serious. Though in many respects the Indians apparently lived more freely and with fewer social constraints than their European conquerors, they nevertheless had strict standards of conduct as far as the welfare of the group was concerned. Many of the stories, especially about the Pleiades, made a point about proper conduct.

The most common theme, however, was escape to the sky, to avoid some earthly trouble. Escape and dancing seem to be natural expressions of the Pleiades around the world.

Some groups, such as the Cherokee of the Southeast, see seven stars, one considerably fainter than the others. Others claim to be able to pick out only six but include in their stories references to a seventh star that has since grown dim. The presence of seven stars in the Pleiades made the constellation especially important to some groups, for they considered the number seven to have ritual or sacred significance. Seven represented the total number of possible directions — south, west, north, east, up, down, and center.

Bright Shining Old Man

This story comes from the Onondaga, who live in upstate New York, south of the city of Syracuse. They were one of the five tribes that made up the Iroquois Confederacy in the seventeenth and eighteenth centuries. The others were the Seneca, the Cayuga, the Oneida, and the Mohawk. Linked by ties of language as well as politics, these five nations lived in the strategically important region south of Lake Ontario. There they controlled the passage of goods and people on Lake Ontario and other smaller lakes. The Onondaga were the "firekeepers" of the confederacy. It was their responsibility to call together the other nations to settle whatever differences had come about during the year.

The Iroquois Confederacy had as one of its symbols the Great White Pine, whose four white roots extend to each of the four points of the compass. The longhouse, where the councils met, was oriented astronomically, with its eastern door facing sunrise and its western door facing sunset. The pillar of smoke from the five fires within the longhouse was thought to pierce the sky above the Onondaga.

Children who dance themselves into the sky are a common theme of the myths of the Pleiades. In this story, going into the sky seems to be a punishment for the children, who found dancing more important than eating. It was also punishment for neglectful parents.

One autumn many years ago, a band of Onondaga Iroquois were walking toward their winter hunting ground near a large lake in southeast Canada. They had to travel slowly, because the land was wild and rough. When they finally arrived at the place they called Beautiful Lake, they were very thankful because, as in years before, they found much game and fish there. Clear water flowed from the many springs in this lovely valley nestled among the hills.

Tracks in the Water, the chief of the band, thanked the Great Spirit for their safe arrival and for the abundance of wildlife. "We will camp here for the winter," he told his people. "It will be a good winter." Everyone was happy. They knew they would prosper in this peaceful valley by Beautiful Lake.

Soon autumn ended and the weather turned colder. Eight children from the band tired of helping their mothers and fathers in the daily chores and began to dance by the lake to amuse themselves. They picked a quiet place away from the village. Each day they met and danced for hours at a time. Though they got hungry and lightheaded, they still danced on and on.

For a long time everything went well. Then one day, while the boys and girls were dancing, a glorious old man appeared to them. He shone like silver in the late autumn sunshine and was covered from head to toe with a cloak of brilliant white feathers. His gleaming hair was very long and white. He was kindly, but he warned the children not to keep on dancing or something terrible would happen to them.

The children didn't want to hear his words; they continued to dance. Each day, Bright Shining Old Man, as they called him, came and warned them, but the children ignored him.

One day the children decided to take food along with them so they could stay out longer the next day. They asked for food, but their parents refused. "You must eat at home as usual. Then you may go play." But they resolved to dance all day long just the same. After a while, the children became hungry, and their hunger made them lightheaded. Then slowly, little by little, they began to rise in the air. Suddenly one youngster cried, "Don't look down, something strange is going on. We seem to be dancing on the air!"

"What great fun!" thought the children. At first they were excited and pleased, but soon dancing on air frightened them. Now they couldn't stop or they would fall to the earth far below. Bright Shining Old Man looked up, shaking his head. He watched them rise farther and farther up into Sky Country.

"If only they had listened to me," Bright Shining Old Man thought sadly.

Soon an old woman in the village noticed that the boys and girls were floating away. She called and called for them to come back, but they did not stop dancing. Then the whole band gathered below and tried to call the children back, but to no avail.

All this time the children kept on dancing faster and faster. They did not look down. One small boy recognized his father's voice above the others. The chief, Tracks in the Water, called loudly to his son, "Come back, come back!" The boy looked down and saw his father. At once he became a falling star. The other children just kept floating up, up, far into the sky. The Onondaga call them Oot-kwa-tah.

Now whenever the Onondaga Iroquois see a falling star, they are reminded of Oot-kwa-tah, the band of headstrong dancing children.

Raccoon's Children and Baby Coyote

Whatever tribe is telling the story, Coyote, the trickster and bungler, can always be counted on either to make trouble for others or to get in trouble himself. Often, as in this story told by the Shasta Indians, he manages to do both. The Shasta, who lived in the mountainous, heavily forested lands surrounding the Shasta and Klamath rivers of northern California, lived by hunting, fishing, and gathering fruits, seeds, and bulbs. Salmon, which they speared, was an important part of their diet. Only a handful of descendants of the three thousand or so Shasta living in the mid-1800s survive today.

Coyote was a major figure in Shasta mythology. He not only played tricks but was often a hero to the Shasta people. For the Shasta, storytelling was an important part of a child's education. Children repeated every sentence after the narrator until they learned a story completely.

Raccoon and Coyote took part in a tribal dance one night. On their way home they noticed a squirrel hole and, close by, its secret back door. Squirrel ran in the back door as Coyote and Raccoon were sitting nearby wondering how to get their supper.

"You take the front door and I will take the back door," said Coyote.

"Reach in and see if you can get him," replied Raccoon.

They both reached in their holes. Raccoon felt sorry for Squirrel and let him escape through the front door while Coyote was reaching farther and farther in the back door.

"I have him!" shouted Coyote.

"No, silly, that is *my* hand you grabbed!"

"It is Squirrel," snarled angry Coyote.

"Stop pulling," begged Raccoon. "You are hurting me!"

But Coyote continued pulling at Raccoon's arm until he pulled it off, killing him.

Coyote went home and told his children to go get Raccoon. "We will have a fine dinner tonight," he said.

The children brought back Raccoon, and pretty soon they were all sitting down to a fine dinner indeed. All, that is, except Coyote's youngest son. His selfish father would not let him share the dinner.

Littlest Coyote was angry as well as hungry. He sat and thought for a while and decided to tell Raccoon's children what had happened. He told them that his father had killed their father. The little raccoons thanked Littlest Coyote and urged him to go back home. They would avenge their father.

The next day, while Coyote was out hunting, Raccoon's children went to Coyote's cave and killed all his children except Littlest Coyote. Then they decided to take him and run away to Sky Country.

When Coyote came home, he could not find his children. Running through his cave, he found nothing. He ran to Raccoon's empty house and searched every room. "Where are my children?" he asked himself.

As he asked this question, he happened to look up toward the sky and saw Raccoon's children and Littlest Coyote rising higher and higher. He tried to follow but could not.

Raccoon's children are the Pleiades. Littlest Coyote is the small star closest to the Pleiades. In the coldest winter, raccoons stay in their holes while the Pleiades shine bright in the night sky. In early summer, when raccoons are out hunting all night, the Pleiades are not visible in the night sky.

Wild Onion Women

Like the Shasta, the Monache Indians of central California also lived by hunting animals and gathering wild plants. As is clear from this story, the women went out picking herbs and other plants while the men hunted. The few Monache who are left today live on the Tule River Reservation in central California.

Many years ago, when the world was new, six young women lived on the outskirts of a village near a large boulder. One day their husbands left to hunt cougar. While they were gone, the six wives also went out, to look for cooking herbs. After searching for a while and digging up an occasional plant with her digging stick, one woman found something new to eat.

"This plant tastes very good," she told the others. "Come and see what I have found!"

Soon all the women were busy eating sweet young onions. They thought the plant so good, they ate and ate until the sky began to turn dark. "We had better hurry home and cook dinner for our husbands," said one woman, and they all went back.

The husbands came home late that night very tired, but they had each killed a cougar.

"What is that terrible smell?" each young man asked as he came to the doorway of his lodge.

"Surely something must be spoiled!" exclaimed one man.

When they bent over to kiss their wives, they discovered where the bad smell came from. Poor husbands!

"We just discovered something wonderful to eat," the wives told their husbands. "Here, taste it," they said happily.

"No! We won't eat those terrible-smelling things," said the husbands. "We can't stand to be in the same lodge as you," they added. "You will have to sleep outside tonight." So the wives slept outside.

The next day, when the husbands left to go hunting, the wives went back to the place where they had found the onions. In spite of their husbands' dislike of the smell, they ate even more than they had the day before. The onions tasted so good that they couldn't help themselves.

When the husbands came home that night, they were tired and angry. "We did not catch any cougar because we smelled like your onions and they ran away. It is all your fault!"

Of course, the wives didn't believe them.

Again the husbands made the wives sleep outside in the cold night air. This went on for a week. The women ate onions and the men got no cougar.

"Go away!" the men shouted. "We can get no cougar with your onion smell on us."

"We can't get any sleep out in the cold," the wives replied.

On the seventh day, the wives took their eagle-down ropes with them when they went to look for onions. One wife brought her baby girl. They climbed the large warm rock near their lodges and rested.

"Let us leave our husbands," said one wife. "I don't want to live with them anymore."

The wives all agreed.

Then the oldest wife whispered a powerful secret word and threw her rope high in the air. It went straight up; it was a magic rope. The middle of the rope hooked over a cloud and the two ends hung down.

The other wives tied their eagle-down ropes to the one hanging from the cloud and called out to them, "Help us, help us, help us!"

Then they stood on the rope ends and sang a special song. Suddenly the ropes began to rise and swing slowly around and around like buzzards in flight. They swung in ever larger circles, going higher and higher.

"Look at the wives floating in the sky," shouted the mothers and fathers as the wives sailed over the camp. "Come back, come back!" they all called.

But the six wives and the little girl kept on swinging from the ropes.

When the husbands came back from hunting, they were sorry they had sent their wives away. The men were not only hungry; they were also lonely.

They decided to use the same kind of magic to get the wives back, so they all hurried to their lodges and brought back their own eagle-down ropes. "We will go after our wives," they thought happily. Their magic was strong and soon they too ascended to the sky.

Now the mothers and fathers in the village were really upset. "Come down, come down!" they called to the husbands. But they kept on circling upward.

The wives looked down and saw the husbands swinging after them. "Shall we wait for them?" one wife asked.

"No! No! They told us to go away. Let's not let them catch us!" the others cried.

"We will be happier in the sky," laughed the little girl.

When the men drew close, the wives shouted, "Stop!" and the husbands stayed right where they were, a little behind the wives.

So the wives who loved onions more than their husbands are all living happily in Sky Country. They are still there today — turned into seven stars. The faintest one of the seven is the little girl.

The husbands did not want to return and are still just behind their wives, a set of six stars called the Young Men [our constellation Taurus].

Baakil and His Five Wives

The Tachi Yokuts lived to the west of the Monache Indians. They too were hunters and gatherers, and subsisted chiefly by fishing on the lakes and rivers of the region. They made rafts or broad-beam canoelike boats out of the tule reeds that grew in the shallow lakes. With the annexation of California by the United States in 1850, their culture began to break down. Like the Monache, their few descendants live on the Tule River Reservation in central California.

Storytelling was an important pastime for the Tachi Yokuts, and included explanations of natural phenomena as well as humorous stories about Coyote and other figures. This story about a flea and his wives has a humorous side that many other Pleiades stories lack.

There were once five girls who were good friends. They sang and played together all day long. No one played with them except a young man named Baakil. Other men wooed the girls and wanted to marry them, but the girls ran away from them. They liked only Baakil, and he was a flea.

Baakil played with the young women constantly and liked them all equally. Because he simply could not make up his mind among them, no one was surprised when he married all five.

One summer Baakil became sick and turned back into a flea. As a flea he made them itch and scratch, so the women did not like him any longer.

"Let us run away," suggested one girl.

"But where shall we go?" asked another.

"He will never find us if we go far to the east," said the most timid.

"When shall we begin our journey?" asked the fourth.

The fifth and oldest girl said firmly, "Just as soon as Baakil takes his nap."

And so they all agreed. When Baakil finally went to sleep, the girls ran away. Wanting to get far away before he woke up, they ran as hard and fast as they possibly could.

They had run a long distance by the time the sun set and the temperature began to drop. The cooler air must have awakened the flea, for he sat up and asked, "Where are my wives?" Baakil soon discovered that they had disappeared, and he set out after them.

"I am faster than they are," he boasted, "and I will catch them!" And before too long, he could see them far ahead.

One of the girls looked back and could see a cloud of dust following them. "Baakil is chasing us," she gasped. "He will soon catch up."

"What shall we do?" asked the timid girl.

"Let us climb up into the night sky. He surely cannot follow us there," suggested the oldest.

Up they went. But the flea rose also.

They became the Pleiades. The girls are the five stars that are close together, and the flea is the one star at the side.

CHAPTER TWO

The Celestial Bear

Stories of the Big Dipper

We call the pattern of seven bright stars that appears to swing continuously around the North Star the Big Dipper because its shape reminds us of a dipper or large ladle. Yet its Latin name is Ursa Major, the Great Bear. It was known as a bear in ancient Greece, where, according to one version of the story, the nymph Callisto, companion of the huntress Artemis, was wooed by Zeus, the king of the gods. Angered that Callisto should accept Zeus' caresses, Artemis changed her into a bear and called her pack of dogs to hunt Callisto down. Zeus, who loved Callisto, took her up into the sky to escape. There she still resides, forever circling the polestar.

The French, the Italians, and the Spanish also knew this constellation as a hunted bear, though the Germans and other Teutonic peoples thought of it as a great wagon. Whatever the image, most stories about the Big Dipper refer in some way to its movement around the North Star.

Because it is nearly always visible in the night skies of the Northern Hemisphere, and because two of its brightest stars serve as pointers to the North Star, nearly everyone is familiar with this constellation. It is usually the first one pointed out to beginners when they are learning to identify the constellations.

The Big Dipper and the Pleiades are the two stellar patterns about which Native Americans most often spin stories, probably because both are easily used as nightly clocks, and both can also help set a yearly calendar. For anyone living above 30 degrees north latitude, the two pointer stars of the Big Dipper also serve as guides to the north. Indeed, because they are relatively bright stars, they are often much more visible than the North Star itself.

Early European travelers must have been astonished to learn that here, as in western Europe, the constellation was often associated with the figure of a bear. The Onondaga, the Cherokee, the Blackfoot, the Zuni, and some Eskimo groups, as well as the Micmac of the Northeast, thought of the Big Dipper as a bear pursued by hunters.

The Celestial Bear

The Micmac Indians lived in the area of the Bay of Fundy in New Brunswick and Nova Scotia, Canada. Before the Europeans arrived, they primarily hunted and fished for food. It is a beautiful but difficult land with a short growing season and harsh, cold winters. Living along the ocean and near numerous lakes and streams, the Micmac developed the construction and use of the birch bark canoe to a fine art. They also used birch bark, carefully stripped from the nu-

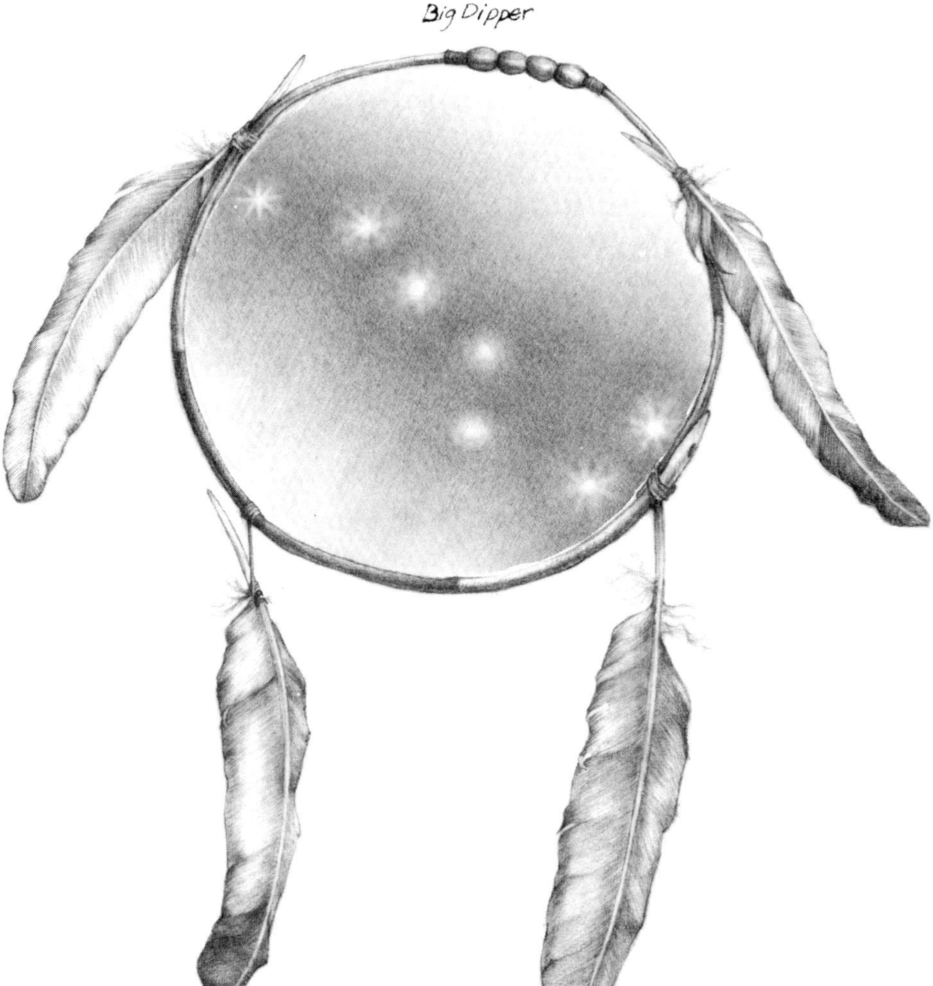
Big Dipper

merous white birches found in their thickly wooded forests, to cover their wigwams.

The following story demonstrates that the Micmac observed stellar movements carefully and applied them to everyday life. At the latitude of the Micmac's homeland, the Big Dipper never drops below the horizon and therefore, on any clear night, easily serves as a clock. The position of the Big Dipper at sunrise or sunset also reveals the round of seasons.

Using the metaphor of a hunt and the habits of animals and birds, this tale describes the passage of the seasons and the movements of the stars. The four stars that make up the bowl of the dipper represent the celestial bear. As you look north in early May, shortly after dark, the bear seems to be climbing out of her den, which is symbolized by Corona Borealis, the circle of stars that appears higher up. In midsummer she runs along the northern horizon, pursued by seven hunters — the three stars of the dipper's handle and four additional, nearby stars. By midautumn the bear stands erect, prepared to defend herself. At this time of year, however, only the three hunters of the dipper's handle, Robin, Chickadee, and Moose Bird (the Canadian jay), always stay above the horizon at the latitude of the Micmac's land. They are the ones the Micmac refer to as "the hunters that are always hunting." This explains why the remaining hunters of the story, Pigeon, Blue Jay, Hoot Owl, and Saw-whet, lose the trail. For several hours of an early-autumn evening, they circle below the horizon and appear to be lost.

Later in the season, when an earthly bear would be fattened up and ready for winter hibernation, the celestial bear appears to be falling over on her back. At this time she is slow and most easily stalked and killed by the hunters. Her blood stains the autumn trees bright red. In midwinter we see her lying on her back as her den reappears in the east, to carry the sleeping new year's bear within. The pot that Chickadee carried to the hunt is the faint star Alcor, which appears next to the middle star of the Big Dipper's handle.

Late one spring day, a huge, lazy mother bear stretched and slowly began to wake herself from her long winter nap. She felt grouchy and hungry as she ambled down the rocky hillside in search of something to eat.

Little Chickadee spotted the bear and grew very hungry himself. Because he was too small to hunt the bear alone, he called six other hunters to help. They soon began chasing the big bear, but not before making sure that Chickadee remembered his cooking pot. So important was the cooking pot that the hunters placed a large bird on either side of Chickadee so he would not fly after some false trail.

The winter had been a long, harsh one, and all seven hunters were hungry as they began their pursuit of Mother Bear. All spring and summer they steadfastly followed her. By autumn, one by one, the slower and heavier hunters, beginning with the two owls, flew lower and lower and began to lose the trail. The next to fall behind were Blue Jay and Pigeon.

Of the seven hunters, the only ones remaining in the chase were Robin, Chickadee, and Moose Bird. These three eventually caught up with Mother Bear in the middle of autumn.

Seeing she had no other choice, Mother Bear turned and reared up to fight the three. Taking careful aim, Robin shot an arrow and Mother Bear fell over on her back. By this time, Robin had waited long enough to eat some bear fat. In his eagerness, he jumped on Mother Bear and became covered with blood in the struggle.

Robin quickly flew to a large maple tree and tried to shake the blood off his brown feather coat. Although he made short work of cleaning off most of the blood, there was one spot on his breast that he could not reach.

"You will have a red breast as long as your name is Robin," shouted Chickadee. And so it is today.

The blood that Robin scattered fell all over the maple tree he was sitting on. Some splashed on smaller trees far below. That is why, every autumn, maple leaves turn the brightest red of all trees.

Chickadee and Robin began cooking the bear meat in the pot Chickadee carried along. But Moose Bird had grown lazy; he had slowed down, knowing the other two would catch the bear and have time to cut it up and cook it. He did not like that kind of work. He arrived just in time for dinner.

Moose Bird thought he was pretty smart to get out of the work and vowed never again to be first in a hunt. "As long as I get my share to eat, I will be happy." And so you see him today, following hunters and eating what they leave. (The Micmac say some men are lazy like Moose Bird and ought to be called by his name, He Who Comes In at the Last Moment.)

Chickadee and Robin shared their meal with Moose Bird. As Chickadee stirred the pot, Robin and Moose Bird danced around the fire to thank the Great Spirit for their good fortune.

All winter Mother Bear's skeleton lay on its back while her spirit entered a sleeping bear. This same bear will amble forth in the spring and be chased and killed by the same seven hunters. And so the story continues year after year.

Grizzly Bear Brother-in-Law

The Coeur d'Alene Indians, who lived in the Plateau country of northern Idaho, also thought of the constellation as a bear — a grizzly. Related by language to some of the Northwest Coast tribes, but by geography and customs to the Plains Indians to the east, the Coeur d'Alene hunted buffalo and other game animals. They were quite familiar with the massive and frightening grizzly bear.

Once there were three brothers who had a grizzly bear for a brother-in-law. The youngest brother liked his brother-in-law, but the other two brothers did not like him at all. In fact they often feuded with him. Yet all had been living rather peacefully for a few months when one day, while they were out on a hunting trip, the two older brothers told the youngest they planned to kill their brother-in-law.

"Do not let him know what we plan," they ordered him.

The youngest brother could not let his brothers kill the grizzly bear, so he crept away from them to warn his brother-in-law. However, the brothers followed close behind him. When he looked back and saw that they were getting their arrows ready to shoot, he acted immediately.

"Look out," he shouted. "They are going to shoot you, Brother-in-Law!"

No sooner were the words out of his mouth than all four were taken up into the sky and transformed into the stars of the Big Dipper. Some people believe that they are the four stars of the bowl of the dipper. Others believe that those four stars are the grizzly bear and that the three brothers are the three stars of the handle.

How Coyote Arranged the Night Sky

The grizzly-bear theme extended southwest to the Wasco Indians, who lived along the Columbia River in Oregon. Though the Wasco lived on the river's abundant supply of salmon and other fish, they were also experienced traders. They and their neighbors the Wishram hosted trading parties from both east and west.

This story links two common themes of Native American mythology — that of a journey to the sky and of the creation of the stars. Here the characters reach the sky on a chain of arrows. This image is particularly common in the Pacific Northwest and the Plateau area.

A very long time ago, when stories were being made, Coyote lived with five Wolf Brothers. Every day the Wolf Brothers went out hunting deer and elk. Every day they brought their meat back to share with Coyote. Every evening as they ate, the Wolf Brothers talked softly together about seeing something strange in the sky. And every evening Coyote became more and more curious.

One night, Coyote could not stand his own curiosity any longer. "What strange thing in the sky are you talking about?" he asked the oldest brother. The oldest Wolf Brother would not tell him.

The next night, Coyote asked the same question of the second-oldest Wolf Brother. "What strange thing in the sky are you talking about?" He would not tell either.

The third night, Coyote asked the third Wolf Brother the same question. He, too, would say nothing to Coyote.

On the fourth night, Coyote asked the fourth brother, "What is it you see in the sky?"

The fourth Wolf Brother would not tell Coyote anything. Instead, he called his brothers together and asked, "Shall we tell Coyote about the strange thing we see in the sky? Shall we tell him what we are talking about?"

"It cannot hurt him or us," said the littlest Wolf Brother.

"Indeed, those two strange things are high in the sky and can do no harm," agreed the second Wolf Brother.

"Let's tell him tonight," said the oldest brother. And so they all agreed.

"We have seen two strange animals high in the sky, but we cannot get near them, Coyote," said the oldest. "This is what we have been talking about each night."

"Well then, let's go see them," said Coyote.

"How can we do that? They are up in the sky," exclaimed the youngest Wolf Brother, impatient with Coyote.

"Getting to the sky is no problem. Come, I will show you how."

Coyote gathered many arrows together. He shot one arrow in the air, and when it reached the sky it stuck there. The second arrow he shot hit the shaft of the first arrow and stuck. His third arrow hit the shaft of the second, then all the rest in Coyote's pile followed, one after the other. Finally there was a long trail of arrows reaching from the sky to the ground.

"Now we wait until morning," Coyote declared solemnly.

Early the next morning, Coyote, the five Wolf Brothers, and their dog climbed the arrow trail. They climbed all day and all night and many more days and nights. At last they reached the sky. There they saw the two animals the five Wolf Brothers had seen when they were hunting. They were two fierce grizzly bears.

Coyote was afraid and warned the brothers, "Stay away from the bears! They will tear you up and eat you!"

But the two youngest Wolf Brothers were not afraid and approached the two powerful grizzly bears. Seeing that nothing happened to them, two more Wolf Brothers followed. The oldest brother stayed back with the dog.

The four daring brothers walked closer and closer, but the two grizzly bears still did nothing. They merely looked at the four Wolf Brothers, who looked back at them. Finally the oldest brother joined them, smiling, with the dog.

"What a lovely picture they all make," Coyote said to himself. "They ought to stay there, to be a story in the sky for all people to come. I will make them stay in the sky."

Quickly Coyote began climbing back down the arrow trail, breaking off the arrows as he went. When Coyote finally reached the ground, the arrow trail was all gone. The five Wolf Brothers and their dog could not climb down.

Every night Coyote went out to look at the story in the sky that he had created. He was pleased with himself.

"Who will know about the story in the sky when I am gone?" Coyote asked himself one night. He devised a clever plan. He told Meadowlark how he had made new sky people. Coyote told him to tell all the people to come what he, Coyote, had done.

That is what Meadowlark is saying when he sings to you at night.

One night Coyote told Meadowlark that there seemed to be too many stars in the sky.

"Yes," said Meadowlark, "and they are growing more plentiful. If too many stars appear, they could fall to earth and freeze everything."

This frightened Coyote. "Look what I started. I must go back to the sky and do something." So Coyote made an arrow trail as he had done before and climbed up once agan.

When Coyote reached the sky, he began arranging the stars in certain patterns. These are the constellations we see each night. Then he spread many out in the Big White Trail [the Milky Way] and told all the stars not to grow too fast. Coyote left the five Wolf Brothers and the two grizzly bears in the same pattern as he had originally pictured them.

The two grizzly bears are the stars that point to the North Star. The two youngest Wolf Brothers are the stars opposite the two grizzly bears in the bowl of the Big Dipper. The older Wolf Brothers are the stars of the handle. The oldest brother stands in the middle with his dog.

The Elk Hunters

Not all tribes associated the Big Dipper with a bear. However, the theme of hunting is an obvious one because this constellation is so visible in the Northern Hemisphere, and because of its constant motion. Hunting requires a reference point, a guide to finding one's way, so hunters would have considered these stars a friend.

In this myth, told by the Snohomish, who lived on the east coast of Puget Sound near the modern city of Everett, Washington, the animal hunted is the elk. Pushing up the sky, or widening the heavens to allow people to live on the earth, is a theme that is often found in Native American mythology. Because the handle of the dipper appears to graze the earth when observed at the latitude of the Snohomish's land, it is easy to imagine that this is how the elk and its hunters climbed into the sky in the north.

When the Creator made this world, he started in the east and traveled slowly westward, giving to each people he created a different language. When he reached Puget Sound, he decided to go no farther. He liked that country. The languages he still had left he scattered all over Puget Sound. That explains why the tribes speak many different languages today.

Although the tribes could not talk together, they had a problem to solve. No one was pleased with the way the Creator had left the sky. In those days, the sky was so low that tall people could easily bump their heads when they stood up. Besides, people in this world could climb trees and go to Sky Country whenever they wanted. Sometimes they could not get back. They decided something had to be done.

One day wise men from each tribe, who had learned one another's languages, met to discuss the problem. They all agreed that the people should get together and push the sky up higher.

"The sky is very heavy," protested one wise man from the east.

"We can do it," said a wise man from the west, "if all our people, even the birds and animals, push at the same time."

"That is a good idea," said the wise man from the south.

"But how will we know when to push the sky up?" asked the wise man from the north. "We all speak different languages. Our people cannot understand each other."

"Let us make up a signal," said the very wise man from the southwest. "Let us use the word 'Ya-hoh.' It will mean 'lift the sky up' in every language."

The wise men went back to their tribes and explained their plan. They all made ready for the big day. Every tribe made long sky-lifting poles from huge fir trees.

When it came time to push, the wise man from the southwest gave the signal. "Ya-hoh!" he shouted.

All the wise men shouted together, "Ya-hoh!"

When the people heard the signal, they all pushed their poles up against the sky. As they raised their poles and pushed, the sky moved a little.

Again the wise men shouted, "Ya-hoh!"

The people again pushed as hard as they could. The sky moved up a little more.

As the wise men shouted again and again, the people pushed. Finally the sky moved to the place it is now. From that day until now, no man or animal has had to worry about bumping his head on the sky, nor has anyone climbed into Sky Country.

A few people, however, had not heard about the project. While the wise men had been planning to raise the sky, three hunters had been out in the woods chasing four elk. Then, just as the pushing-up began, the elk had all reached a place where the sky touched the earth. The hunters pursued them as they leaped into Sky Country. They all rode up with the sky.

Soon they turned into stars. When you look up at the Big Dipper on a dark night, you can still see the three hunters chasing the four elk.

CHAPTER THREE

Coyote Scatters the Stars

Myths from the Southwest

The stark desert landscape of the Southwest, home of the Navajo and the Pueblo Indians, leaves an indelible impression on the visitor. In the summer enormous, puffy cumulus clouds tower above the rugged sandstone mesas, offering hope of rain that seldom falls to wet the earth. On the mesas, against a backdrop of subtle tones of pink, yellow, earth red, and gray, stand short piñon and juniper trees and the ever-present sagebrush. In this land you can see for miles with few obstructions. At night the sky reaches down to touch the earth in all directions, holding many more stars than you can count.

The Pueblo Indians take their name from the Spanish word for town. They live in villages made up of clusters of box-shaped buildings. The Navajo, by contrast, prefer to spread out and live in small family groups. The Pueblo are known as farmers, tending their small fields of corn, beans, squash, peaches, and melons with great care. The Navajo, though they too plant and tend some crops, focus most of their attention on raising sheep and cattle. Both groups must work hard to thrive in the high desert, where water is so scarce. They have learned to watch the sun and the stars for information about when to plant and when to harvest. Though their language, customs, and traditions are quite different, both groups consider the sun, moon, and stars sacred, and use these celestial bodies to guide their lives.

Black God and His Stars

To live in the traditional Navajo way is to live, in part, according to the ways of the stars. Families build their winter home, the hogan, according to the sky-related plan that the gods gave the Navajo after they emerged from the underworld. They build one form of the traditional hogan with a frame of five poles placed in the four astronomical directions — one each in the south, west, and north, and two smaller ones in the east. As they work, they sing songs of the First Hogan, which was built by First Man. The builders start by leaning the east poles into place in the earth. Working in the same direction as the sun travels through the sky, they next set the south and west poles into the earth. These poles lean against the east poles. Finally the north pole slips into place to hold them all. Then, after placing the doorway facing east to let the first rays of the rising sun shine through the hogan door, the builders enclose their house. As they explain, "First Man covered the poles of the First Hogan with sunbeams and rainbows. We use tree limbs and earth."

When the hogan is complete, the family blesses their new home and sings the blessing song. Family members place a pinch of cornmeal on each of the four main beams — passing from the east around to the south, west, and finally north — and sing, "May it be beautiful, my house." Upon entering their hogan, they walk around to the south (that is, to the left). The Navajo term this "walking sunwise," because that is the direction the sun and stars follow in moving through the sky. Sunwise is the proper way to enter a hogan.

Wintertime is storytelling time for the Navajo, and the right place to tell the old stories is in the hogan. When the ground is frozen, families gather to hear the old legends. They relax on thick sheepskins spread across the floor, warm and safe from harsh weather, and listen to grandfather, grandmother, or a favorite uncle or aunt retell the familiar stories. The following tale comes from the Navajo creation myths and tells about the Beginning Time. Like most other Native Americans, the Navajo do not group the stars into patterns in the same way as early European astronomers did.

In the days before the stars were made, the Navajo gods of creation met in their hogan to discuss how to make the world and what to put in it. Black God joined them after the others had arrived. Attached to his ankle he carried the small group of stars called Dilyehe. Several of the other gods noticed the stars and asked what they were. Black God said nothing, but wishing to display his power, he stamped his foot hard four times, once for each direction: south, west, north, and east. With the first stamp, Dilyehe jumped to his knee. Black God stamped a second time and the stars jumped to his hip. The other gods nodded approvingly. Another hard stamp brought them to his shoulder. A fourth and final stamp of his foot caused Dilyehe to lodge along his left temple. "There," he said, "it shall remain!" And there it still remains. Today, when Black God dances in the Navajo ceremonies, this small constellation is always painted on the left temple of his mask.

The other gods asked Black God to fill the dark night sky with stars to make it beautiful. He took out a pouch that he always carried with him, made from the skin of a fawn. Opening it, Black God took out a single bright crystal. He reached far out into the sky and carefully placed the first crystal precisely in the north. It became North Fire, the star that never moves, which guides the nighttime traveler. All other stars move around this star.

Next he picked out seven great pieces of crystal and placed them near North Fire. This constellation he called Revolving Male, because it circles North Fire. After this, Black God placed another set of stars near North Fire — Revolving Female. Both she and Revolving Male always circle North Fire. Most other stars remain beyond the nightly path of Revolving Male and Revolving Female.

Black God now turned to the east. Taking out five bright crystals and reaching toward the eastern sky, he placed them in a pattern the Navajo call Man with Feet Spread Apart.

Then he reached to the south and created First Big One. Black God made three stars below it called Rabbit Tracks, because they look like the

Little Dipper

tracks a rabbit leaves in the snow. In the south and around to the west he placed the constellations Horned Rattler, the Bear, and Thunder.

Black God placed several other constellations in the sky. Then he carefully made a copy of Dilyehe, the stars on his left temple, to put in the sky. Finally he reached into his fawnskin pouch, produced thousands of tiny crystals, and spread them across the sky to make Which Awaits the Dawn.

After Black God was finished creating the star patterns, he placed in each of them a single igniter star to light up the crystals. When he had completed this part of his work, Black God then started to sit down and admire what he had done. But before he could, Coyote, who was always hanging around looking for trouble, approached the group of gods. "See here, what are you doing? You didn't ask my advice!"

Coyote was a trickster, and the other gods didn't like his pranks, because he often meddled with their carefully organized plans. Black God answered, "You can see for yourself what I have done. Look at all the beautiful patterns I have created. These patterns will provide humans with the rules to live by on earth."

Black God, who always sat with his legs crossed, protected his fawnskin pouch by placing it under his foot. This time, before he could be stopped, Coyote quickly reached for the pouch and snatched it away. "Here, let me help you," he said with a grin. Then, opening the pouch, Coyote blew the remaining crystals across the sky. He scattered thousands of points of light in a disordered jumble.

There they remain today. Only the patterns that Black God placed so carefully now have names. The ones Coyote blew at random into the sky are nameless, except for a single star. After he had emptied the pouch and scattered its contents, Coyote looked inside. "There is one crystal left. It shall be my star!" Then, mimicking Black God's placement of North Fire, he took that crystal and set it in the south. Today it is called the Coyote Star. It is also called the Monthless Star, because it appears only for a few days in the year, far to the south.

Black God scolded Coyote for disturbing his arrangement of the stars and leaving so much chaos and disorder in the sky. Coyote just laughed.

Tossing the fawnskin pouch back to Black God, he said, "Now the skies are beautiful!"

Some star patterns tell stories. The seven stars called Dilyehe are said to be the Hard Flint Boys, who play a game of dodge and shoot as they pass through the night sky. Years ago, when young Navajo boys practiced their fighting skills so they could successfully raid other tribes, they would play such a game, using bows and blunt arrows. Each boy would shoot and at the same time sidestep arrows shot by his friends. One of the hardest parts of this game was to knock one's bow with the next arrow while dodging the flying arrows. In the sky, six Hard Flint Boys dodge and shoot while their littlest brother follows behind them. You can tell which direction the boys are traveling by locating the brother who follows.

The Navajo call the night sky the Dark Upper. By placing Dilyehe where he wanted it, Black God proved to the other gods assembled in the hogan of creation that he had the power and the knowledge to create patterns in the sky to guide human behavior. By scattering some stars, Coyote transformed the sky into a realm that is less orderly and predictable, more like life on earth. According to Navajo thought, our task as humans is to find the harmony between the orderly and predictable world, represented by Black God, and the unpredictable, represented by Coyote.

By observing how the positions of the stars change through the seasons, and how the stars disappear and reappear again, the Navajo have developed a highly practical stellar calendar. They watch various star patterns to know when to plant and when to harvest.

Even young children learn the cycle of the seasons by watching constellations change position. They discover that when Revolving Male is standing straight up, at about nine o'clock on early-spring evenings, it is time to prepare the fields for planting. Later on, in May and early June, Revolving Male lies on his side, and the Navajo know that it is time to complete the planting of corn, beans, and squash, their staple foods. In the early fall, when Revolving Male slants down to the east, it is time to harvest the crops, for winter will soon arrive. Some Navajo also watch Revolving Male to tell them when to start certain ceremonies, or when certain animals will mate and bear young.

The Navajo also use the patterns Dilyehe and First Slender One (part of Orion) to help them schedule their planting. First Slender One follows Dilyehe across the sky. When we can see Dilyehe overhead in the early evening, it is January. Then First Slender One's head is just to the east of Dilyehe, and his feet nearly reach the eastern horizon. We see First Slender One to the west in the early spring. To the north (right) of First Slender One is a curved line of stars that represent a digging stick. Above them is a small circle of stars making a basket filled with corn seeds. When the Navajo see First Slender One setting at twilight, they know it is time to plant.

Just after Dilyehe disappears from the western sky in the spring and First Big One (part of Scorpius) appears, the Navajo know that spring will soon be over. Then, when they can see Dilyehe in the east for the first time, around the summer solstice, they know it is too late to plant.

The Navajo learn as young children to make a string figure of Dilyehe resembling a cat's cradle. Such string games are fun to play, but like many games, they also teach. According to Navajo lore, Spider Woman taught them to make Dilyehe and other string figures so they would learn their relationship with the stars, the sun, and all of nature. If Spider

Woman catches you in her web, they say, she won't let you go until you make all the figures —Dilyehe, Big Star, Two Stars, Coyote, Owl, Butterfly, and the others. You are supposed to make such string figures, and tell the stories, only in the winter, when the spiders sleep and cannot see or hear you. If you play string games in the summer, Spider Woman will cause harm.

Spider Woman, who is a helpful spirit as long as you follow the Navajo way, taught Navajo women how to weave rugs, blankets, and clothes. According to legend, her husband, Spider Man, taught them how to make their looms. He fashioned the First Loom from parts of the sky and the earth. First Spider Man made the warp sticks from sun rays. The cotton warp he made of spider web. Next he tied the warp to the upper warp pole with strings of lightning and to the lower warp pole with strings made of the sun's halo. The cross poles that supported the warp sticks he made of sky and earth. Spider Man used the sun's halo for the loom's batten, and its comb he made from white shell, the symbol of sunrise.

The Little Girl Who Scatters the Stars

Pueblo villages are clustered along the Rio Grande in central New Mexico and in the two western Pueblo reservations of Hopi and Zuni in Arizona and western New Mexico. Although they sometimes use the Pleiades and Orion as stellar clocks during the winter months, the Pueblo people are much more familiar with the movements of the sun. The sun is their principal deity, the source of warmth and growth. Nevertheless, they tell a few stories about the stars.

This tale is from Cochiti Pueblo, which is located beside the Rio Grande, south of Santa Fe. In telling about the origin of the stars, it relates the familiar theme of curiosity and the temptation to look into forbidden places. The result is chaos, though Kotcimanyako, the little girl of the story, seems not to be punished for her transgression, perhaps because the storyteller considered curiosity and chaos too much a part of our world to punish the child who brought them.

The mother of the story is the mythical being whom the

Cochiti consider the mother of their pueblo. According to another Cochiti myth, she and her younger sister quarreled. Her sister challenged her to a contest. "Tomorrow before the sun comes up we shall each pick a place to stand. Whoever receives the warmth of the sun first shall be the greatest." The younger woman felt sure of winning because she was taller. Yet when the sun rose, his rays shone first on the first-born. The younger sister was furious and challenged the older one to kill her. But when the older sister threw a rabbit stick at her, the younger one turned into a wood rat and disappeared into the rocks. The older sister became the mother of the Pueblo people, and the younger one became the mother of the Navajo.

The story mentions three constellations: the Slingshot Stars, the Pot Rest Stars, and the Shield Stars. Of the three, we can associate only two with European constellations. The Slingshot Stars are the same as the constellation Delphinus the dolphin. The Shield Stars are the Big Dipper. The Pot Rest Stars remain unknown to us.

Long ago, in the days after the great flood when all things began to come alive again, the people emerged from the underworld. They began moving slowly to the south as they were instructed by Our Mother, the mother of the Pueblo Indians. She also told the people that they were all brothers and sisters and were to live as one large family.

As they began traveling, one little girl, Kotcimanyako, was left behind in all the hustle and bustle of packing and moving out. She stood looking up at Our Mother.

"Come closer, Kotcimanyako," said Our Mother.

The little girl came closer, and Our Mother gave her a little bag of tightly wrapped white cotton.

"Carry this little bag on your back," she told Kotcimanyako. "Do not unwrap the bag for any reason."

The little girl promised not to open the bag.

Again Our Mother said, "Be very careful, little one, and remember not to open the bag no matter what happens."

Again Kotcimanyako promised, though she had no idea what was in it and did not know why she was forbidden to open the bundle.

And so Kotcimanyako began on her journey to the south, hoping to overtake the others before too many days passed. As she walked she wondered about many things, but most of all about the bag on her back. "Why can I not open the bag? Would it hurt to take just a little look?" And so she thought until her head was spinning and her curiosity began to get the better of her.

At lunchtime she took the bundle off her back so she could rest by a little stream. She asked herself, "One little peek couldn't hurt anything, could it?"

The bundle was tied with many knots. It seemed to be growing in her hands as she struggled with the first knot. Before long she came to the last one and began working it loose. Just then something popped out. As the knot fell apart, more things flowed from the bag and scattered all over the sky. She had no idea what they were, but they were coming out so fast that she grew very frightened.

Quickly she tried to grab the ones that had not flown away and stuff them back into the bag. Her nimble fingers worked fast to gather as many as possible. Then she put them in her bundle and tied it tightly.

When Kotcimanyako came to the south and the end of her journey, she discovered that the things she had let out were stars. She unwrapped the few stars she had been able to keep and the elders placed them in their proper patterns. This is the reason why most of the patterns are unnamed — those are the ones that scattered when Kotcimanyako opened her bundle. The few we have names for are the ones that remained in her bag. They are the Slingshot Stars, the Pot Rest Stars, and the Shield Stars.

Coyote Scatters the Stars

The Cochiti tell at least two other versions of how the stars came to be. In this one, as in the Navajo tale "Black God and His Stars," a meddlesome Coyote scatters the stars. This story also explains why Coyote has had bad luck ever since.

In the Beginning Time, when the people came up from the underworld, there was a great meeting of all the four-legged and flying people. When they were all gathered together, Our Mother chose one man to put the stars in the sky and name them. Then she pointed to a jar in a corner of the meeting house and turned to Coyote and told him, "Do not take the top off that jar."

The chosen man began to arrange the stars in ordered patterns. He placed the Seven Stars and the three stars making up the Pot Rest Stars. Then he very deliberately added Morning Star to the sky and stood back from the jar to admire his work.

Even then, Coyote was no different than he is now. He could not stay still even for a few minutes. And he was the most curious of all the people. Finally he could stand it no longer. He looked around and saw that Our Mother was not watching, so he said to himself, "I think I will peek into that jar in the corner and see what that man was doing."

Coyote crept over to the corner while everyone was admiring Morning Star and slowly lifted the top of the jar. Before he could raise the lid enough to peek inside, all the stars jumped out and scattered. That is the reason why so few star patterns are named.

Our Mother saw what Coyote had done and grew extremely angry. "You have done much mischief here today. From now on, Coyote, you will be a wanderer and get into trouble wherever you go. Some days you will be happy and have plenty to eat, and some days you will be unhappy and go hungry." She opened the door to the underworld and all the animals spread out in all four directions.

The Dove Maidens

In the pueblo of Picuris in northern New Mexico, the winter, when the earth sleeps, is the time for telling stories. In one story, two Dove Maidens give their crops to the Picuris so "they will not do so much hunting," and "that they may learn to work." Unfortunately, we do not know which stars the two Dove Maidens became.

Once upon a time, two sister Dove Maidens lived with their ancient grandmother at Picuris. Every day all the village maidens ground corn — except the two Dove Maidens, that is. They sat with the grandmothers of the village and wove baskets.

One bright sunny day, the two Dove Maidens watched sadly as the others laughed and chatted together. The cornmeal powdered the maidens' faces as they ground.

"Why do we not grind corn?" one Dove Maiden asked.

"Why do we have to sit and make baskets with the grandmothers?" the other Dove Maiden asked.

"We want to grind corn like the other young maidens," they both implored.

"Oh, please, do not say that!" exclaimed their grandmother, bursting into a flood of tears. But she would say no more.

"Get corn ready for us, Grandmother. We will grind corn tomorrow," the maidens told her stubbornly.

The grandmother said nothing. That night she toasted the corn in readi-

ness for grinding, weeping all the while. The granddaughters could not understand why she was weeping, and she would not, or could not, tell them.

Bright and early the next morning, the two Dove Maidens took their grinding stones and joined the other maidens. While they ground, they sang a little song. The Dove Maidens soon began to rise slowly in the air. Though they rose higher and higher, they continued to sing happily and grind their corn.

Looking up, their grandmother cried, "Please stop grinding. Please do not sing that song. Please stop and come back." But the two sisters continued to rise. They kept grinding happily and singing all the while.

"Stop grinding corn and come back!" pleaded their old grandmother. They continued to grind and sing, and they continued to rise.

The Dove Maidens soon disappeared from sight. That night, however, when the stars came out, the grandmother pointed to two new stars just rising over the mountains. She gathered the village maidens together and pointed to the stars. "See what happened to my two granddaughters?" she scolded the maidens. "This is a reminder to you all to obey your parents."

The maidens all looked up above the mountains and saw the two new stars. Now, when girls want to stay strong grinding corn, they pray to the two Dove Maidens.

SOUTHWEST STARS AND STAR PATTERNS

Navajo star or constellation	*Western equivalent*
Bear	Unknown
Coyote Star	Possibly Antares
Dilyehe	Pleiades
First Slender One	Part of Orion
First Big One	Upper part of Scorpius
Horned Rattler	Unknown
Man with Feet Spread Apart	Corvus
North Fire	Polaris
Rabbit Tracks	Tail of Scorpius
Revolving Male	Big Dipper
Revolving Female	Cassiopeia
Thunder	Unknown
Which Awaits the Dawn	Milky Way
Cochiti constellation	
Pot Rest Stars	Unknown
Shield Stars	Big Dipper
Slingshot Stars	Delphinus
Picuris stars	
Dove Maidens	Unknown

CHAPTER FOUR

When Stars Fell to Earth

Legends of the Pawnee

The Pawnee Indians, like the Navajo, were keenly aware of the stars and their movements. In some places, the grassy plains of Nebraska, where the Pawnee lived and hunted buffalo, stretch for miles in all directions without a tree or hill to obscure the vision. On a clear night, the canopy of stars wraps around you like the solid earthen lodges the Pawnee lived in.

One group of Pawnee, the Skidi, or Wolf, Band, especially revered the stars and watched them nightly for guidance in daily living. They believed that the stars carried the wisdom of Tirawahat, the Pawnee's supreme being. Tirawahat lived directly overhead in the zenith. From him came everything in the world, including the stars. The Skidi believed that some stars were sacred spirits. Others were people who had lived on earth in the past. Unfortunately, few descendants of the Wolf Band are alive today to tell us about their starlore. What we know of their stories comes from the efforts of a few men and women who were determined to write down as many Skidi Pawnee myths and folklore as they could before they were lost forever.

Even as children, members of the tribe learned about the exploits of the star spirits and heard stories about the Skidi constellations. On a winter evening, surrounded by the walls of their lodge and warmed by the coals of a hot fire, families would listen to the Pawnee elders as they told the ancient stories.

The Skidi esteemed the planets too, which they believed were stars possessing strong powers. Mars they called Morning Star, and Venus was Evening Star, even though either planet can appear in the morning and evening skies at different times of the year. They looked to Morning Star for advice and direction in their affairs. Dressed as a powerful warrior, Morning Star often appeared to Pawnee warriors in

their dreams and counseled them to perform acts of bravery and daring in battle.

The Skidi learned much from watching the sky. They scanned the heavens nightly, looking for clues about how the tribe should live. They watched with particular care the movements of Morning and Evening stars which re-enacted their mythical courtship and marriage: slowly but surely, Morning Star and Evening Star moved among the other stars until Morning Star overtook Evening Star and made her his wife.

As the Skidi Pawnee story describing this sky journey goes, Morning Star won Evening Star by overcoming numerous star monsters she placed in his way, and by completing a series of tasks she set for him. Four of the monsters were bright stars called the beasts of the four directions — Black Bear, Mountain Lion, Wild Cat, and Wolf.

After conquering them, Morning Star said to the sky beasts, "You four stars will stand at the four corners and hold up the heavens." Turning to Black Bear, he said, "Black Star, you are to stand in the northeast, where night comes from. Your season is autumn. Yellow Star (Mountain Lion), you will stand in the northwest, where the sun sets golden. Your season is spring. White Star (Wild Cat), you must take your place in the southwest, looking north in the direction of the snow. Your season is winter." Last, Evening Star looked directly at Wolf and said, "Red Star, your place is the southeast, and your season is summer."

Skidi elders also told this legend about the four stars: Before the First Earth Lodge was built to house the First Children, the four directional stars came down to earth to place the four posts that would hold up the roof of the lodge. "Remember us by these posts," said the stars to the First Children. "We will help remind you in which direction to find us, to make offerings to us." From then on, the Skidi always painted their lodge posts according to the colors of the stars.

As the Skidi elders explained to their children, the earth lodge was patterned after the sky. Whenever the Skidi built a new lodge, they built it like the First Earth Lodge. The roof was domed in imitation of the sky; the circle where the roof met the earth represented the horizon, which they could see all around them on the wide-open prairie. The smoke hole represented the star group called the Circle of Chiefs (the constellation Corona Borealis). The Pawnee elders told the children, "During the month of May you can watch the Circle of Chiefs pass overhead at midnight. They remind us of the first council of stars that Morning Star governed."

When the First Earth Lodge was being built, explained the elders, Morning Star appeared in the east in the first light of dawn and told the Pawnee, "Build your lodge so the doorway faces east. East is my home. It is the source of light and warmth."

You can imagine what it must have been like to grow up in a Skidi earth lodge, living in a model of the sky. Even from inside the lodge you could figure out the directions on earth and in the sky. All around were the symbols from the sacred stories about the star spirits, which meant so much to the Skidi Pawnee people.

Skidi legends don't tell us which stars are the four directional stars. The Skidi considered knowledge of that sort sacred; only a few holy men could identify them. However, astronomer Von Del Chamberlain, who has studied Skidi Pawnee starlore, suggests that Black Star is Vega and White Star is probably Sirius. Yellow Star is perhaps Capella, while he believes Red Star is Antares. For all but Black Star, the colors of the directional stars Chamberlain identifies correspond to the Pawnee names.

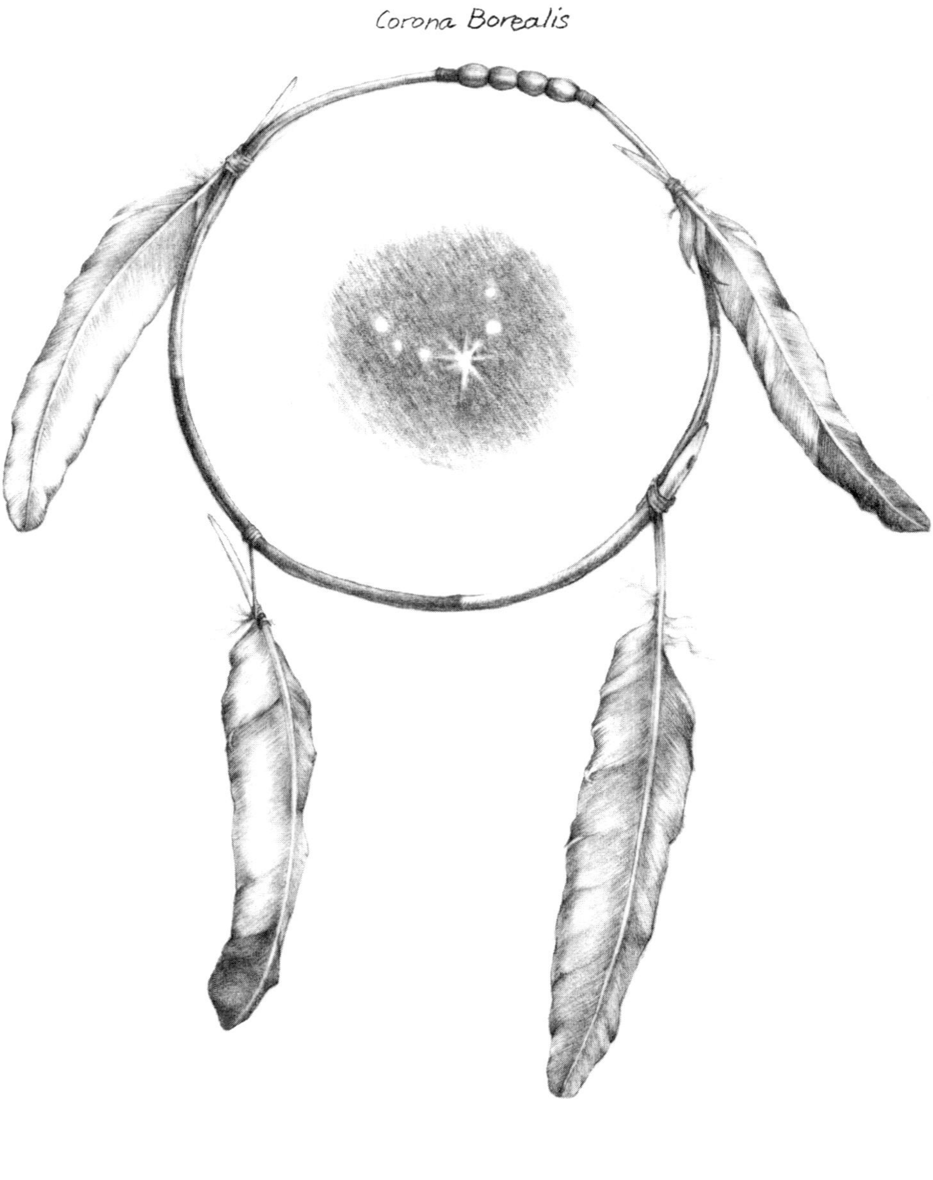
Corona Borealis

Stone God

> In explaining how the Skidi Pawnee might have chosen the name Black Star for a bright white star like Vega, astronomer Von Del Chamberlain suggests that at one time, many years ago, the Skidi Pawnee might have witnessed a large, bright meteor streaking to earth from the northeast, the direction from which Vega rises. When a meteor breaks up, it drops many small meteorites that fall to earth burned by the heat of friction in the atmosphere. The Skidi Pawnee venerated the blackened rocks because they thought of them as children of Tirawahat, star spirits who brought wisdom and good things to the Skidi. The following story tells about one warrior's encounter with such a star spirit.

In the days when buffaloes roamed the plains, a young Pawnee warrior, Osage Sky Seeing, was riding over the prairie when nighttime overtook him. The night was dark, for the moon had not yet risen, making travel difficult as well as dangerous. So the young man decided to lie down and sleep until the moon rose to give him light.

As he slept, he dreamed that he saw a star fly across the sky, making a long, bright trail behind it. It looked like a pony's tail flowing in the wind. His dream so startled him that he woke up immediately. There before him he saw the very shooting star of his dream coming nearer and nearer. The bright star seemed to fall very close to where he lay.

As we sometimes do when we are startled out of a deep slumber, the young man soon fell back to sleep. When he awoke again, the sun was about to rise. Looking around, he found the fallen-to-earth star near him. It was a very dense, shiny black stone. Thinking that the stone might bring him luck, he wrapped it carefully and tied it to his belt. Then he continued his journey.

When he made his camp the next night, the warrior dreamed again. This time he dreamed of a handsome young man whose face was nearly as dark as the night sky. The man of his dream had a bright star painted on his forehead.

"I am the stone that fell beside you," he said to the sleeping warrior. "I came from a star in the southeast. Carry me with you in all your travels."

Osage Sky Seeing stirred in his sleep, but the dream-speaking star-man continued to talk to him. "Take me with you whenever you go on a journey or venture out to find wild ponies. Put me in front of you before you begin such a journey. Perform a smoke ceremony. Fill your pipe and smoke first straight above, then to the other stars, and then to me. When I flicker brightly in the sky, you will know I am with you to make your adventure successful. Remember what I have told you."

When the warrior awoke, the moon was high and he continued his journey to the camp of his people. After dawn he gathered around him all the elders of the tribe and told them of his dream and of the star-stone. The whole camp held a smoke ceremony. The elders wrapped the star-stone very carefully in a beautifully tanned buckskin bundle. Into this sacred bundle they placed downy eagle feathers and laid the star-stone on top. Then they tied it with rawhide and put it in a special place.

Before the end of the summer, the young men wanted to ride out and capture more ponies for their families. The elders put the bundle with the star-stone before them and offered smoke once more. Osage Sky Seeing again dreamed of the star-man. The star-man spoke to him. "Ride east to the land of the sun. You will find many ponies there. They are waiting for you to bring them back home."

Tying the bundle to his belt, the warrior mounted his horse and guided the other warriors toward sunrise. The men rode till they reached the Arkansas River. Along the way they captured many ponies. Osage Sky Seeing found a beautiful young stallion that promised to be a good runner. He led the pony home and took good care of him. It became Osage Sky Seeing's special horse, which he always rode when he led the young men of the tribe on raids.

Whenever the tribe needed more horses, they asked Osage Sky Seeing to bring out the star-stone bundle and dream again of the star-man. Each time, the star-man told them where to search. Each time, they were blessed with many ponies. The tribe prospered thanks to the dream-speaking star-man, who told them where to find ponies.

The Pawnee Constellations

According to the Pawnee, the chief of the stars was the Star That Does Not Walk Around (the North Star, or Polaris). He guided the movements of the other stars. He also watched over the earth and its people and was considered to be the first chief of the constellation called Council of Chiefs.

Beyond the Star That Does Not Walk Around you can see the two star patterns the Pawnee thought of as stretcher-bearers who carried the sick and the dead. Large Stretcher (Big Dipper) was made up of four stretcher-bearers and three stars that followed — Medicine Man, his wife, and Errand Man. Little Stretcher (Little Dipper) was also known as Small Stretcher Bearing a Sick Child. As they traveled through the sky, the Star That Does Not Walk Around watched over them.

The Skidi Pawnee thought of the Milky Way as the path the spirits of the dead take as they are blown along from north to south by the north wind. They explained that, because most people linger in sickness before they die, their spirit path is long and corresponds to the long trail of the Milky Way. The spirits of people whose death came suddenly, in battle or by accident, travel a shorter path.

Although we know little about Skidi Pawnee constellations, we do have some information about the stars the Skidi priests used to set their yearly calendar. Even as children, the Skidi Pawnee learned how to tell the seasons by the stars.

The Skidi marked the two halves of the year with the stars

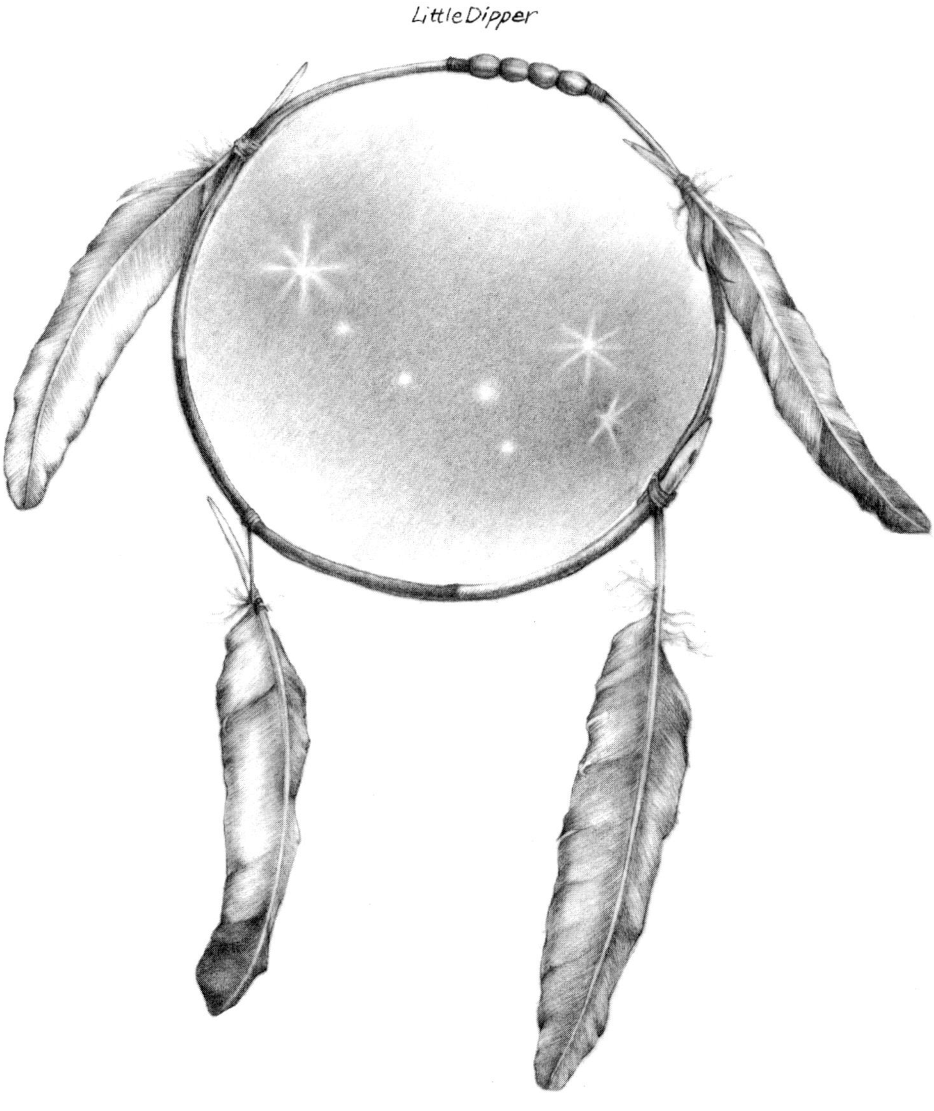
Little Dipper

known as Swimming Ducks and the South Star. When Swimming Ducks first appeared just before dawn, twinkling in the southeast, the Skidi knew that spring and the time of thunder were not far away. They thought Swimming Ducks represented loons that rose late at night in the spring to tell the water birds to fly north again. The Skidi also believed that the arrival of Swimming Ducks was a signal to sleeping water animals to awaken and break through the ice. The elders would say, "The two duck stars are now swimming in the pond." Swimming Ducks brought thunder and lightning, which caused the spirit of life to awaken in living things and the earth to renew itself.

After studying all the evidence he found for the identity of Swimming Ducks, astronomer Von Del Chamberlain has concluded that it is the two stars at the tail of the constellation Scorpius. This pair, Lambda and Upsilon Scorpii, annually become visible in the southeastern sky for the first time in February. As the year progresses, you can watch them move higher and higher until April, when they reach their highest point in the sky just before dawn. By mid-August you can see Swimming Ducks reach its highest point about an hour past sunset. By late November, when most of the animals on the Plains are hibernating and the birds have flown south, Swimming Ducks disappears from the night sky. The Skidi Pawnee ceremonies were then also at the end of their yearly cycle.

According to Skidi tradition, the South Star ruled the winter. No one today is quite sure which star the Skidi called the South Star. Some say it was Canopus, the second-brightest star in the sky. Yet Canopus is too far south to be visible from the Pawnee homeland in Nebraska. Von Del Chamberlain thinks the South Star may have been Sirius, the same star that was also called the White, or Southwest,

Star. Sirius is an excellent candidate for the South Star because it first shines in the east just before sunrise in late August. Its appearance at that time would alert the hunters out seeking buffalo that it was time to return to the earth lodges and harvest the crops they had planted in the spring. By the time Sirius disappeared from the night sky in the spring, Swimming Ducks would have made its appearance.

Like the Navajo, the Skidi Pawnee watched the Seven Stars (the Pleiades) for clues about when to plant and harvest. In late winter, when Swimming Ducks had just become visible, the Pawnee religious leaders would look through the lodge's smoke hole to watch the Seven Stars pass above them. When they could no longer see the Seven Stars through the smoke hole, they knew it was time to prepare the fields. This was in late February. When the Seven Stars became visible again, just before dawn, the holy men knew that it was time to harvest. It was then mid-September.

The Seven Stars were particularly important to the Pawnee, as they were for most Native Americans and other peoples of the world. The Pawnee even had a song for the Seven Stars:

Look as they rise, up rise
Over the line where sky meets the earth.
Seven Stars!
Lo! They are ascending, come to guide us,
Leading us safely, keeping us one.
Seven Stars,
Teach us to be, like you, united.

The Seventh Star

According to the Skidi, the Seven Stars represent six brothers and an adopted sister whom they rescued from a frightening rolling skull. Here is one version of that story.

The spring was especially warm and beautiful on the Great Plains, home of the Pawnee. Sunshine and a gentle breeze made the days delightful. The nights were blessed by clear skies and a bright moon. Game and water were plentiful and the people lived content. It seemed nothing could mar their peace.

A beautiful young Pawnee woman was walking happily just outside her lodge one warm day. When she looked up, she saw a cloud of dust approaching. As the cloud reached her feet, it stopped abruptly. When the dust settled, she saw a rolling skull. Before she could jump out of the way, the skull grabbed her and began to pull her away from camp.

"Let me go," the young woman screamed as she fought with Rolling Skull, but no one came to her rescue.

She tried to resist as he dragged her along, but it was no use. The skull was too strong. After a long time they both collapsed. By then they had covered many miles, and the woman knew she was far from home. There was no chance of running into a band of hunters or warriors. What was worse, she didn't know how to get back. But she had to try!

Rolling Skull finally grew tired and yawned. The young woman pretended to be sleepy herself. They both lay down for a rest.

When Rolling Skull was fast asleep and snoring loudly, the young woman crept quietly away. She ran and ran, hardly noticing where she was going. She ran through groves of trees and over brooks, through grassy clearings and over rocks. Suddenly a mysterious-looking old man dressed in strange clothes walked up to her and asked, "What are you afraid of? Why

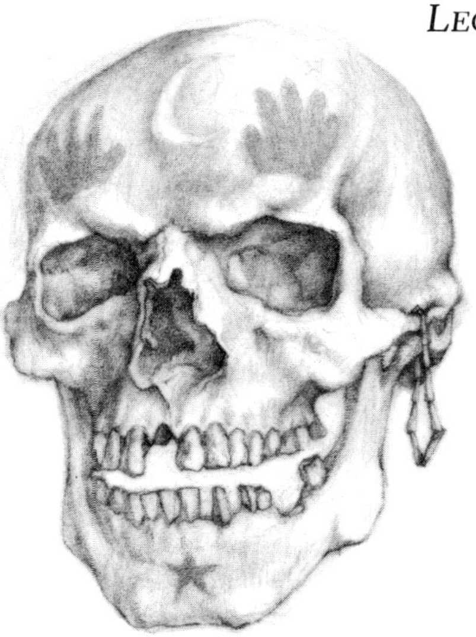

are you traveling alone and so far away from the protection of your own people?"

She was too astonished to answer him. After a long silence, he added quietly, "Can I help you?" She began to cry softly and tell her story.

The following day, the old man took her to a tiny lodge belonging to six brothers. They called her Little Beautiful One and took good care of her for several days. Still she was afraid. She stood on the doorstep and looked out each day, searching for the cloud of dust that would announce Rolling Skull's presence. One day as she stood outside the cabin staring at the horizon, she saw what she feared most.

Rolling Skull had finally caught up with her! He roared up to the lodge, furious. "I have found you at last!" he shouted to her when the dust had settled. "I have captured you, and you are mine!"

This made the brothers very angry, for they had grown quite fond of Little Beautiful One. They were not about to let her go with Rolling Skull. In the few days she had been with them, the brothers had devised a plan for killing the skull and saving the young maiden. But would their plan work?

"She wants to stay with us," the third-youngest brother called to Rolling Skull from the doorstep of the lodge.

"She is our sister now," called the second-youngest brother, dancing up to and kicking the skull.

"You cannot have her!" shouted the littlest brother, throwing stones at the skull.

As the three younger brothers argued with Rolling Skull, the three others crept out the back door and came up behind the skull. They hit him with a huge pole and broke him into pieces. And so they saved her. The young woman was very happy and lived peacefully with the brothers for some time.

One fine night when they were at dinner, she asked them, "Where are we, brothers?" for she could recognize no landmarks. It seemed to be very far from her camp.

"This is Sky Country," the second-oldest brother told her. "We live here all by ourselves and are very lonely."

"Yes," said the second youngest, "we have all talked together and want you to stay with us forever and be our sister."

"Will you stay with us?" asked the youngest, tugging at her clothing.

"I would be honored to be your sister and would be happy to live with you," said Little Beautiful One. And so she did.

Now, the brothers are the six brightest stars in the constellation called the Seven Stars. The young woman became the seventh star. The three older brothers play on her right side and the three younger brothers play on her left side. You can see them in the sky on any clear winter night.

Basket Woman, Mother of the Stars

The Skidi Pawnee's interest in making the stars part of their lives extended even to their games. Pawnee women played a game in which plum seeds decorated with symbols of the stars and the moon were used as dice. One woman would place the seeds in a shallow basket. Then, tossing the seeds lightly in the air, she would slap the basket to the ground. The women taking part in the game would bet with each other on which symbols would fall face up.

Even the basket was related to the sky, for it represented the moon, which during the creation was the basket Tirawahat used to send the stars to earth. The stars, who were the children of Basket Woman, brought knowledge to the people. The Skidi had a story that tells how the basket "dice" game started.

Back in the Beginning Time, when all things were being created, First Man lived in a forest of tall pine trees. One day while on a hunting trip, he discovered a small lodge. Next to the lodge was a tidy cornfield. "I wonder who lives here?" he thought. The next day, First Man brought his wife, First Woman, through the forest to see the lodge.

As they came near, a little old woman came out to greet them. "I am Basket Woman, or Moon, the mother of the stars. I lured you here." Then she invited her visitors inside. Around a small fire sat four old men: Wind, Cloud, Lightning, and Thunder. The lodge was filled with Moon's daughters. Soon the girls began to sing and dance. Moon's daughters told First Man to watch and listen carefully so he could teach the sacred songs and dances to others.

After the singing and dancing, Basket Woman's daughters taught First Man and First Woman ceremonies and games. Evening Star danced in the west and held a basket representing the moon. The basket was made of willow reeds held together with mud, for the earth is filled with trees.

Four daughters of Black Star were also there. They danced and moved toward the west, and each placed what she carried in Evening Star's basket — two swan necks and two fawnskins. These represented the four gods in the west.

Then Basket Woman's daughters taught First Man and First Woman a game. They gave them the moon-basket; plum seeds, which represent the stars; and twelve sticks, which are the Circle of Chiefs in the sky. They used the sticks as counters. All this they taught to First Man and his wife to remind them that Tirawahat sent the stars to earth in a moon-basket to teach these first two everything that people were to do.

When First Man and First Woman had learned all they should, their neighbors from the lodge jumped into their basket and flew up to the sky to return to their places.

White Elk, the Bear Man

Other Pawnee bands, closely related to the Skidi, had their own star stories. The following tale was told during the bear dance of the Pitahawirata, one of the Pawnee's South Bands.

In the days when animals could speak, a man named White Elk wandered into a den of bears. The bears decided to teach him their mysteries and send him back to his own people full of new knowledge and power. Bears have always possessed great mysteries and powerful magic.

While White Elk was living with them, he received the gift of the bear spirit. With this special gift, he could understand the bears as though they were speaking his own language. They taught him many practical things and invited him to learn certain sacred songs.

The songs they taught him were about Morning Star. Each morning before the sun rose, the bear family shambled from their cave. They faced east and sang to Morning Star. White Elk followed them. When he looked around the sky, he saw that the stars were dancing and twinkling. While the bears sang, he gazed happily at the dancing stars.

After sunrise the bears returned to their cave. Each day, their leader taught him the songs they had sung. He also told White Elk that the songs were sacred and must be sung at a certain time if their power was to work. Morning Star rises in the early dawn, he explained, and that is when his song must be sung. When White Elk sang the songs, the leader of the bears told him to ask for anything he wished from Morning Star and it would be granted.

The bears' leader then showed White Elk the dances that go with the Morning Star songs. When he returned to his people, White Elk took the songs and the dances back to them. With their help, his people prospered

for many years. They sang the Morning Star songs and danced the Morning Star dances.

White Elk wanted to remember his time with the bear family, so he painted his tipi in a new way. First he painted Morning Star on the back, with cedar trees on each side. Then White Elk painted a bear standing up on either side of the cedar trees. Ever afterward the Pawnee painted their tipis with this powerful symbol.

PAWNEE STARS AND STAR PATTERNS

Star or constellation	*Western equivalent*
Morning Star	Probably Mars
Evening Star	Probably Venus
Black Star (Northeast)	Vega
White Star (Southwest)	Sirius
Yellow Star (Northwest)	Capella
Red Star (Southeast)	Antares
Star That Does Not Walk Around	North Star
Large Stretcher	Big Dipper
Small Stretcher	Little Dipper
Circle of Chiefs	Corona Borealis
Swimming Ducks	Lambda and Upsilon Scorpii
Seven Stars	Pleiades
Path of the Dead	Milky Way

CHAPTER FIVE

Morning Star

Legends of the Plains Indians

Many of us, when we conjure up an image of the Native American, bring to mind the Plains warrior, feathered headdress flying in the wind, racing into battle upon a charging horse. That image is so strong partly because most Plains tribes waged a dramatic war with the early settlers who were moving into their traditional hunting grounds. Their feats of stealth and daring became the stuff of modern legend. Eventually they succumbed to the superior weapons and numbers of the settlers, but not until the encroaching non-Indian hunters and commercial traders had killed off the herds of buffalo upon which the Plains tribes depended so heavily for food, clothing, and shelter.

We know of more than twenty distinct Plains tribes, including the Blackfoot, Cheyenne, Pawnee, Kiowa, Mandan, Crow, Dakota, Assiniboin, Omaha, and Comanche. Before the white men arrived, most Plains tribes lived a nomadic life as hunters and gatherers but without benefit of the horse. When they moved from place to place to find better hunting grounds, or to gather ripe berries and seeds, they had only dogs to help.

The dogs carried the tipi lodge poles and covers strapped to their backs or on travois. The people, including women and children, walked from camp to camp. The men did all the hunting, even buffalo hunting, on foot because they had no other choice. This limited their movements and forced them to carry only small lodges and few household implements from place to place.

We will never really know what those "dog days" were like, however, because the arrival of the horse changed the lives of the Plains Indians dramatically. The horse must have brought changes equivalent to those made two hundred years later in American society by the automobile. Soon after they obtained their first few horses, the Plains tribes became entirely dependent on them for transportation, for hunting, for prestige, and for barter. Now they were able to extend their range of travel for hunting and raiding.

With the blanket of stars stretched out around them on clear nights, and with an unobstructed horizon, it is not surprising that most Plains tribes developed a strong interest in

the stars. Bright stars and certain constellations became markers of direction, nightly clocks, and seasonal calendars, all at one time. Warriors considered the celestial bodies sacred beings of great power and often painted images of the sun, moon, and stars on their war shields. Morning Star was especially important to the Plains groups. As the following Blackfoot story about the origin of the North Star relates, they thought of Morning Star as a being who could occasionally take human form.

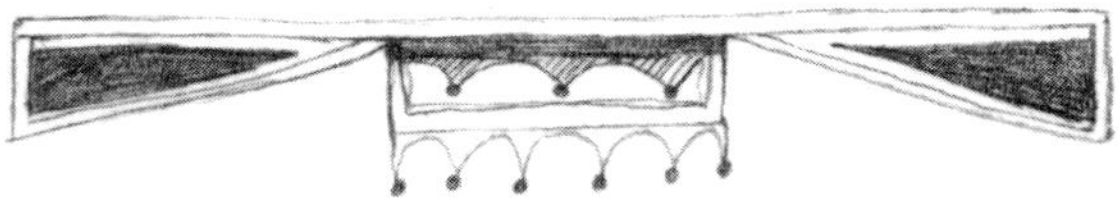

The Fixed Star

Tipis, especially those of the Arapaho, Blackfoot, and Kiowa, were often painted with celestial symbols. The particular design of any tipi generally originated in a dream or vision of the owner. Bears, deer, porcupines, and other animals, as well as celestial symbols, were used. One strikingly beautiful nineteenth-century tipi, owned by the Kiowa warrior Black Magpie, was called Star Picture Tipi. Black Magpie painted the south half of his tipi red and the north half blue. Nearly 120 circular disks representing stars covered the two halves of the tipi. Like the Blackfoot woman of the following story, Black Magpie also placed Morning Star in the shape of a cross on both the north and south sides of the tipi.

One hot summer night in Montana, two Blackfoot sisters decided to sleep outside their lodge. The sky was clear and there was a warm breeze; the young women went to sleep quickly. Sometime before dawn both of them awoke and gazed at the beautiful night sky and the early-morning stars.

Looking toward the east, one maiden pointed out Morning Star to her sister. "That star is so beautiful. He is winking at me. How happy I would be to have him for a husband."

As the sun came up and the day broadened, the tasks of the day soon grew upon them, and both young women forgot the night's talk.

Several days later, the sisters walked out to gather firewood. They picked up sticks, made up their packs, and tied them on their backs with strong leather straps. They were cheerful and chattered happily as they went. Soon the strap on one of the bundles broke. It was that of the girl who had wished for Morning Star. Each time she retied her bundle, the strap broke again. Her sister said, "I'll go on ahead. After I unload my firewood, I'll come back and help you."

The first maiden kept trying to fix her bundle of firewood. Finally she decided to wait for her sister. When she looked up from her task, she found a handsome young man watching her. He was dressed all in fine beaver skins and wore a tall eagle feather in his hair. The young woman started to hurry away but he stopped her. "What do you want of me?" she asked him.

"You said you wanted me for your husband, and here I am," he replied.

"You are a stranger to me. Why would I want you for a husband?" she asked, startled. "I don't even know you!"

The young man laughed and replied, "One night you looked at me in the sky and said you wished to have me as your husband. I am Morning Star. I have come to take you as my wife."

The next moment, the handsome youth gently took her hand. They smiled at each other as he removed the feather from his hair. "Shut your eyes," he told her and placed the feather in her hair. They rose up into the sky.

When the young maiden opened her eyes, she was in the house of Sun and Moon, the youth's mother and father. She was not afraid, but she did feel a little confused because she had seen no place like this before. "Come and meet my wife," Morning Star called to his parents. "Make her feel at home in Sky Country."

Moon fed the girl four berries and a little water in a shell. The four berries, one for each direction, symbolized all the food in the world, and the water in the shell represented all the water in the oceans. She could not finish her meal.

After she had eaten, Moon took her aside and said, "I have something special for you." She gave her a root-digger and showed her how to gather roots, warning her not to touch a certain turnip. "This turnip is special to the gods. It is a sacred turnip," Moon explained. "Evil will come to us all if it is touched."

Now, this turnip was very large, and the young woman often looked at it when she was out digging for roots. She wondered, "What would happen to me if I dug that turnip up? Why is it so special?"

Many happy days came and went for the young woman and Morning Star. After a while, she gave birth to a baby. Each day she went out to gather vegetables for the evening meal. Each day her curiosity and desire to dig up the turnip increased. One day she sat the baby outside to play and decided to go out alone and dig up the turnip. The turnip was big and the earth was hard. Her root-digger got stuck in the ground. She grew afraid and tried to pull it out, but it would not budge. She sat down and started to cry.

Crane Man and Crane Woman were flying overhead and heard her crying. When she saw them, she prayed to them, "Please help me."

Crane Woman said, "I have been a good and faithful wife, so I have much power to help you. Your mother-in-law gave you the root-digger. I will teach you the songs that go with it. They are special and will help you." Crane Woman burned incense and sang. Soon she pulled out the root-digger and, dancing around the turnip, made three thrusts with the digger. With the fourth try, she pulled out the turnip. "Take your root-digger and your turnip home," Crane Woman said.

As she was leaving, Morning Star's wife looked at the hole Crane Woman had left when she pulled out the big turnip. She thought she could see something moving and looked a little closer. "I can see my people and my old camp," she thought. She felt sad to see everyone down there working so hard while she was happy and living at ease in Sky Country. It was the first time the young woman had been sad during her stay in Sky Country, the first time she had missed her people.

Morning Star and Sun and Moon were extremely unhappy when they saw what she had done. They asked her if she had seen anything when she pulled out the turnip. "I saw the camp and hunting grounds of my people," she replied.

Morning Star shook his head and told her that she would have to take the baby and go back to the Blackfoot people. "It was wrong to dig up the sacred turnip. Sorrow has come to Sky Country. I cannot keep you now," he said. "When you return to your people, do not let our baby touch the ground for fourteen days. If he does, he will turn into a puffball and return to me. Then he will become a star."

The woman did not want to leave her husband, but she longed for her own people more. Sun called an old man to help return the woman to her people. The man brought a strong spider web. "I will tie you and your son to one end and let you down through the hole in the sky," he told her. So the old man let her down the turnip hole and right into her own camp.

"Here is the woman who went to the sky," some boys called when they saw her. "She has come back." Soon the whole camp came out to greet her and look at her baby.

Before the woman left Sky Country, Morning Star had told her to paint a morning star symbol on the back of her lodge, so she would remember her mistake in digging up the turnip and not make another mistake and let the baby touch the ground. She did this and watched the baby very carefully for thirteen days.

On the fourteenth day, the woman's mother said, "I am tired. Will you go get water for our lodge? I will watch the baby." The young woman agreed but warned her mother against letting the baby touch the ground — although she did not tell her why. The grandmother left the baby on the pallet a few feet away and was humming and doing beadwork in the sunlight. Now, the baby had just learned to crawl and wanted to play in the sunlight. He very quietly crawled off the pallet. Just as he touched the earth, he turned into a puffball and got tangled in a robe. The grandmother turned around and saw the bundle squirming. "He is asleep," she thought happily.

Soon the mother came back. "Where is my baby?" she asked.

"I just checked him. He is asleep in the robe," the grandmother answered.

The mother turned to pick up her son. In his place she found only a puffball.

That night a bright new star shone in the sky. The puffball had risen and stuck in the hole in the sky where the woman dug up the turnip. This is why that one star never moves. The Blackfoot call it Fixed Star.

The grief-stricken woman went home and painted circles all along the bottom of her lodge to represent the puffball her son had become.

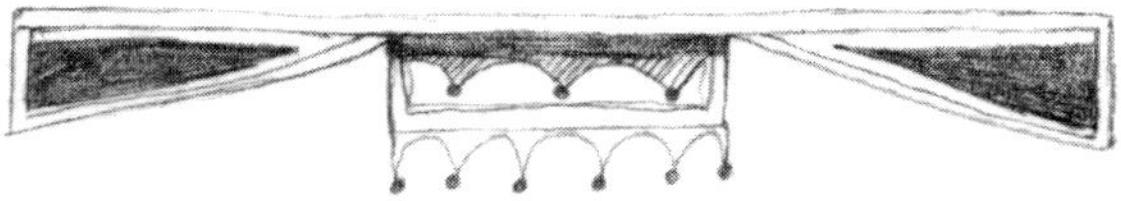

The Sacred Pole

The power that came from the sky and the stars figured in Plains tradition in a variety of ways. The Omaha, who lived on the plains of Nebraska, symbolized that power by means of a sacred pole, which, when it was displayed in ceremonies, was pointed toward the north celestial pole. It represented the center of the four directions, and because it pointed toward the Star That Does Not Walk Around (North Star), it also represented the imaginary axis of the earth. Although it may seem strange to us, the Omaha thought of this pole as having very special powers, and they treated it as if it were a human being. According to Omaha tradition, at a time of crisis in the tribe, the power of the pole helped to keep the tribe together.

Many, many years ago, the bands of the Omaha tribe began to go their separate ways. The tribe had become very large, and each band now had its own customs. The chiefs decided they needed a way to keep the tribe powerful. All the bands met in council for many days. Everyone agreed that something had to be done, but no one could agree on just what to do.

As the elders met, the son of one chief was off hunting. Returning home at night through a great forest, the young man lost his way. After fighting the underbrush for some time and finally losing his sense of direction, he stopped to rest. As he sat, the young man gazed upward through the trees to locate the North Star. "If I can find the Star That Does Not Walk Around," he thought, "I will at least know the way back to camp." As he looked around, he saw a light through the woods. Thinking that it came from a tipi hearth, he walked toward it. "Perhaps I am not so far from home after all," he thought.

When he reached the light, he stared in wonder at a flaming cedar tree. Its trunk, branches, and leaves were glowing as if the whole tree were afire, yet the tree did not burn up. It gave off neither smoke nor heat. He was even able to touch the tree without burning his hand. This was a mystery. He sat down to watch the tree. All night long the tree remained lighted; only with the coming of dawn did the tree's strange light fade. When daylight arrived, the tree turned green again.

Thinking that this tree might be a special sign to his tribe, the young man stayed nearby and waited. As the day wore on, however, he grew less sure of what he had seen. When the sun finally set and night approached, he watched as the tree became luminous again. As before, he could touch it without burning himself. He stayed near the tree through another night. After the sun rose once again, and the tree was green again, he marked the place and walked toward camp, which was near a lake some distance away.

When he reached his home, he sat with his father and explained all that he had seen. That night his father followed him to the place. As the young man had said, the trunk, the branches, and the leaves all gave off a beautiful light.

The father noticed something about the tree that his son had missed:

four animal paths, one from each direction, led to it. Each track was well beaten. Examining the area more carefully, he saw that the animals had rubbed against the tree, polishing its bark. What he saw made him realize that in this tree could be the means of keeping the people together. He told his son, "The Thunderbirds, alighting from the sky, make the trail of fire that lights up the tree. The power of the sky is within it."

Father and son hurried back to the camp. The father sent for the chiefs and proclaimed, "My son has found what we have searched for in the form of a miraculous cedar tree. The Thunderbirds descend from the sky above, making a trail of fire that lights it up. They also leave four paths, burned into the grass, stretching in the four directions. When the Thunderbirds alight on the tree, it seems to burn but is not consumed. During the day, it becomes a green tree again."

The chiefs sent runners out to examine the marvelous tree. When they returned, they told the same story. The chiefs held a council with all the people, and after mulling over what the tree might mean to them, the chiefs decided, "This has come as a symbol of unity for us. Just as the tree is the center of the four sacred directions, it shall be the center for the people." Then, speaking to the warriors, they said, "Prepare yourselves as if for battle. The tree is powerful and its light comes from the same thunder that brings us strength for war. It deserves the greatest honor."

The men painted themselves and dressed for battle. They raced to the tree and attacked it as if it were a worthy enemy. The first warrior to reach the tree struck it once. Then all the others counted coup on the tree as well.

After they cut it down, four men hoisted it up on their shoulders and carried it back to the camp. For four nights the chiefs sang songs about the tree and held a council. They decided that because the tree had special spiritual powers, like some humans, it should be treated with reverence. They made a tipi for the tree and decorated it with round red spots to symbolize the sun. They set the tipi within the circle of lodges. The chiefs trimmed the tree so it became a pole, and made a basket pouch to tie around its middle. Then they tied a scalp lock to the top of the pole.

They painted the pole red and erected a large ceremonial enclosure made from poles selected from the lodges of the tribe. Only valorous men were allowed to select the poles. Each man went to a tipi and, after entering, struck a pole as he recounted his deeds. Everyone then helped to set up the poles in a semicircle that opened north. They covered the poles with buffalo hide. It became a holy lodge representing all the people.

Then, after singing sacred songs, the keeper of the Sacred Pole set it before the holy lodge, leaning the pole on a crotched stick and pointing it in the direction of the Star That Does Not Walk Around.

When everyone from the tribe was gathered together before the Sacred Pole, the chiefs said, "The pole that you see here belongs to all the people. He is a great mystery that we welcome. Whenever any of us meet misfortune we shall bring our troubles to him. With our prayerful requests we shall also bring gifts."

Before the people scattered, they agreed to gather each year during "the moon when the buffaloes bellow" (July) to commemorate the gift of the Sacred Pole and to anoint it with fresh red paint.

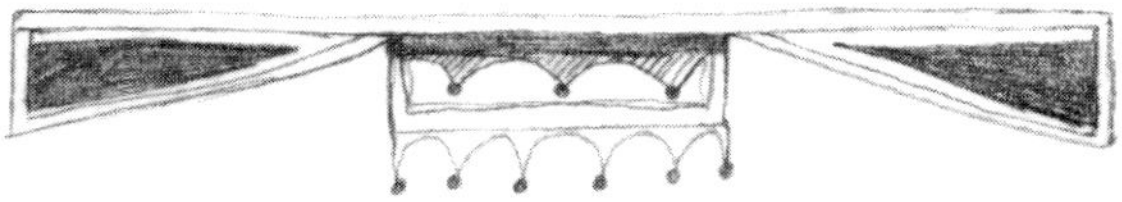

The Sun Dance Wheel

The stars, the four directions, and the sky played important roles in some Plains games. In the Pawnee basket dice game, for example, the dice represented the stars, and the basket represented the moon. Other Plains tribes, including the Dakota Sioux and the Omaha, also used dice marked with the moon and the stars.

In the game of hoop and pole, played in one form or another by nearly all the Plains groups, the hoop represented the path of the sun through the sky. The hoop was most often marked at each of the four quarters. Three players took part in the game; one rolled the hoop while the others ran after it and threw two sticks at it. The contestants tried to strike the hoop in such a way that both sticks would fall either over or under specific marks, which they called out as they threw their sticks.

In some tribes, hoops were an important component of sacred ritual. The Arapaho, a tribe related to the Cheyenne and the Blackfoot, performed a Sun Dance ceremony every summer in which a hoop like the game hoop was displayed prominently on the Sun Dance altar. The Arapaho generally held their Sun Dance when the tribe reassembled after being dispersed in separate bands for the winter. The Arapaho associated the hoop with a creation myth that explained the origin of major elements of the Sun Dance ritual. One part of the myth described the creation of the Sacred Wheel and explained its parts. The disk of the wheel represented the sun, while the band of wood from which it was made symbolized a harmless water snake and represented the water that the Arapaho believed surrounded the earth. The markings at each of the four quarters were the signs of the Four Old Men, spirits who ruled over the four cardinal directions and controlled the four winds. Blue beads tied to the wheel represented the sky, and the eagle feathers tied to it symbolized the Thunderbird, who brought the rain. As a whole, the wheel stood for all of creation — the sun, earth, sky, water, and wind.

We do not know the corresponding, familiar names of some of the Native American constellations mentioned in this story. Often the anthropologist writing down a story had little knowledge of the stars, was more interested in the tale than in astronomical data, or did not know what to ask of the storyteller. Sometimes the storyteller considered the information about the stars sacred and would not reveal it to the questioner.

At one time, water covered all the earth. No land could be seen in any direction. It was then that a man walked across the water for four days and four nights, thinking. In his arms he carried Flat Pipe, his only companion and good counselor. The man wanted to treat his pipe well and give it a good home. For six days he fasted while he thought how to do this. Finally on the evening of the sixth day he reached a firm conclusion. "To give Flat Pipe a good home there should be land, and creatures of all kinds to inhabit it."

On the morning of the seventh day he resolved to find land. Calling in all directions, he asked the animals to help. And from the four directions came all manner of animals willing to offer their aid. It took a long time, but finally, with their help, he made the earth a home for Flat Pipe and placed the Four Old Men in the four directions to control the winds. The earth was also to be the place of the Sun Dance Lodge, where every year the people would gather to worship together, praying for bounty and health for the tribe.

The man saw a tiny snake and said, "Come and sit near me, Garter Snake. You will be a great comfort to the people in the future and will have an important place in the Sun Dance Lodge. You will be the Sacred Wheel." Then, looking around to the many helpers that had gathered nearby, he said, "We will need material for a wheel."

Many offered, but Long Stick, a bush with flexible limbs and dark red bark, was most suitable. He said, "For the good of all, I offer my body for the wheel. I am anxious to do good. Please accept my offer so my name will live through the ages." All murmured approval, and they made Long Stick into the ring for the Sacred Wheel.

Then the eagle spoke up, saying, "My great strength and power carry me high above the earth. My holy body and broad wings soar on the winds of the four directions. I offer my feathers as symbols of the Four Old Men. From here on, if anyone should give you eagle feathers to honor and respect, please remember this day and my request. Help them use my feathers well."

The man then said, "Eagle, the good and faithful one, has asked that his feathers be used to represent the Four Old Men. We will honor his desire and tie four bunches of eagle feathers to the wheel."

After he had shaped the Sacred Wheel, the man painted it in the image of Garter Snake and arranged the eagle feathers in the positions of the Four Old Men — northwest, northeast, southeast, and southwest — and tied them carefully. Then on the wheel the man placed Morning Star, the Pleiades, and Lone Star. Next he placed other groups of stars, such as Chain of Stars, Seven Buffalo Bulls, the Hand, the Lance, and the Old Camp. Finally he painted on the Sacred Wheel the symbols of the sun, the moon, and the Milky Way. The man thanked Garter Snake, who was pleased to serve the people in this way.

The Seven Stars

In the following Assiniboin legend, our familiar name for the "seven brothers" is not mentioned. The story itself contains some important clues. Because it refers to two rows of three stars with a little star in the middle, we believe that the story is about the Pleiades.

Deep in the northern Plains there lived seven brothers who were all alone in the world. They wondered if they had parents or not. Every lonely day they trudged along, looking for their home. All they ever got from their search was, in summer, sunburn and scratched arms and legs from bushes and low growing trees, and in winter, frostbite and empty stomachs. They had great difficulty finding food and warm clothing.

One afternoon in early autumn, the littlest brother, Red Hair, sat playing with a web he had borrowed from a friendly spider. He turned and asked the others, "Why don't we change ourselves into something else? Then we might be happier. The wind may blow and snow may grow deep but that won't disturb us. Best of all, we won't have to wander and go to sleep hungry."

"That's a good idea, but what shall we change ourselves into?" they all asked.

One suggested, "How about earth? Earth is solid."

The brother they called Wise One replied, "No, not earth. Rain turns earth into mud and earthquakes can cave it in."

"What about rocks?" suggested another, hanging upside down from a nearby tree limb.

"Don't be silly. Rocks fall and get broken up."

They all sat for a long time, thinking under the forest's big trees — thinking about change, stability, and growth. Bright autumn leaves fell all around them, covering last year's tracks and burrows and tender young shoots with a blanket against the snows to come.

"Big trees do not get broken to pieces," one brother suddenly said. "They just bend in the wind."

"Even big trees," reminded Wise One, "are blown down by storms and fierce winds."

"We could change into water," piped up the quietest brother. He had been floating bright leaf-boats in the swift-flowing brook by their side. The last rays of the sun played on the leaves and turned the water to molten gold.

"No," said one brother. "Don't you know? Water dries up in summer and is destroyed. We don't want to dry up, do we?"

They all shook their heads seriously. Surely they did not want to dry up.

"How about night? Why don't we change into night? Night is never destroyed."

"Night fears sunlight and runs away from the day," replied Wise One.

"We can change into daytime then," another offered.

"Day and night chase each other," explained Wise One. "And they take turns destroying each other."

By now the afternoon had faded into night. Stars began to show their bright faces in the darkness.

"Sky Country never changes," said Wise One, looking up. "We can change into stars. Stars live up there and never change or die. They fear nothing. Sky Country never dies. Let us go live in Sky Country!"

At last the brothers resolved what to do. There would be no more arguing. They would now have a home forever in the sky.

The littlest brother, Red Hair, hoisted them all up to Sky Country with the help of his spider web. Once there, he placed three brothers on one side of him and three on the other side. Red Hair sat in the middle. They still sit that way in Sky Country.

PLAINS INDIAN STARS AND STAR PATTERNS

Star or constellation	*Western equivalent*	*Tribe*
Star That Does Not Walk Around	North Star	Omaha
Lone Star	Evening Star	Arapaho
Old Camp	Corona Borealis	Arapaho
Seven Brothers	Pleiades	Assiniboin
Morning Star	North Star	Blackfoot
Fixed Star	North Star	Arapaho
Chain of Stars	Unknown	Arapaho
Seven Buffalo Bulls	Unknown	Arapaho
The Hand	Unknown	Arapaho
The Lance	Unknown	Arapaho

CHAPTER SIX

They Live in the Sky

Stories of the California Indians

The Chumash tribe, who lived in the rich coastal area around Santa Barbara in southern California, enjoyed telling stories about the natural world. Many were about the sun and moon, the stars and planets. Like the other California tribes, the Chumash kept careful watch on the heavens in order to track the seasons and divine the weather. They thought of the stars and planets as First People, who came from the time before humans were created, and who had ascended to the world above to evade death. As one member of the Gabrielino tribe, neighbors of the Chumash, said: "Those who did not want to die escaped to the sky, and that is why all the stars have names. While all who remained on earth are mortals, those who went to the sky always live."

The Chumash and their neighbors lived by hunting, fishing, and gathering seeds and plants, rather than by planting and harvesting crops. The mild climate of southern California and the abundant supply of wild plants, fish, and game made it possible for them to have ample leisure time for sacred ceremonies and storytelling.

The Chumash had a highly structured society in which the keepers of starlore were respected and feared by the common people. By the time anthropologists and others began collecting their legends, most of the knowledgeable men and women had died. The stories were taught to anthropologists by their friends and relatives. Therefore, we know relatively little about Chumash starlore, but what we have learned tells us that it once must have been exceedingly rich.

The Land of the Dead

The Gabrielino Indians, who lived near the Chumash and shared many customs with them, told a story that illustrates how the common man learned about the stars. Because he had watched the experts carefully, he was able to complete a task set for him by spirits in the Land of the Dead.

Once, a man who had lost his wife was so stricken with grief that he decided to follow her to the Land of the Dead. Her spirit, which had become invisible, warned him, "No one has ever followed a spirit where I am going. It is extremely dangerous." Nevertheless, he insisted on going with her as she traveled the Road of the Dead.

Eventually, after crossing a broad sea, they reached the Land of the Dead, where they were greeted by voices that complained, "Why have you brought that earthly substance? Take him away."

Though the husband heard the voices, when he looked about he could see nothing at all — not even his wife.

The wife pleaded with them. "Please let him stay. He is much better than most men. Besides, he is an excellent hunter and can help you."

Finally the voices relented. "We cannot let him stay, as he would never be happy here, but if he can complete four tasks, you can return to earth with him."

The man's first task was to retrieve a feather from the top of a long pole. He was frightened. The pole was so tall he could barely see the top of it. His wife comforted him. "Don't worry. The pole is very long, but if you don't look down, you can reach the top without falling."

He climbed and climbed and was careful not to look down. The voices applauded him. "You are very good at climbing," they said.

Next they gave him a hair to split. It was extremely long and he was doubtful about completing the task. His wife encouraged him. "Just have faith in yourself and you will do it." It happened as she said.

His third task was to draw a map of the sky, showing the Big Dipper and the North Star. He was now more frightened than ever, for although he had watched the tribal wise men make a sky map for certain ceremonies, he did not know how to do it himself.

His wife helped him remember what he had seen, and he was successful. The spirits were pleased with him. "Well done," they said. He had completed three of the four tasks.

Finally, they required him to hunt deer for them. They sent along four of their number to help him drive the deer out of the ghostly trees. But when the spirits who accompanied him cried out "there they are!" he could see nothing.

He returned dejected, and the spirits jeered his efforts. Nevertheless, they let him try again. But he was no more successful the second time than the first.

His wife begged them to let him try a third time. "I know he is a very skillful hunter. Please let him try once more."

When the spirits agreed, she turned to her husband and said, "This time you must kill some deer."

"But how can I kill deer if I can't even see them?" he complained.

"You must have seen some black beetles when you were out hunting. Those are the deer," she said.

He thanked her and started out again. This time when the spirits cried "there they come," he was prepared. He stabbed at one of the many beetles that crawled across the ground. Instantly a slain deer appeared before him.

He killed more and more beetles until the spirits urged him to stop. Then they said, "You have shown us your prowess as a hunter, and you have made a map of the sky. You have split a long hair and retrieved a feather from a tall pole. You may return to earth again, and take your wife as well. However," they continued, "you must not touch her for three days. If you do, a great misfortune awaits you."

The grateful husband agreed and turned back toward the land of the living with his still invisible wife behind him. When they left the spirit realm, he would look back every so often to see if she was visible yet. But he could not see her, though her voice was strong.

The first night back on earth, after he had built a fire and lain down, he finally began to make out a faint shadow across the fire from him. On the second night, she became easier to see. Finally, on the third night, his wife appeared before him as she had before she died. He was so overjoyed to see her whole again that he forgot the spirits' command. He reached out to embrace her, but all he held was a log. The man lamented his mistake, but he could do nothing. He wandered sorrowfully for the rest of his days.

Sky Coyote

The Chumash called the North Star the Star That Never Moves. They also considered it the star that separates the sky. If you draw an imaginary line south from the North Star, you divide the sky exactly in two. For half the day the sun is east of this line. During the second half it is west of the line. The Star That Never Moves may have represented the celestial being the Chumash called Sky Coyote. They regarded Sky Coyote as a helpful creature who looked after the people. Sky Coyote opposed Sun, who often captured young children during his daily travels and took them home for him and his wife to feast on.

Every year Sky Coyote and Morning Star played a gambling game called *peon* with Sun and the giant Sky Eagle. At the winter solstice, they counted up points to see who had won for the year. When Sky Coyote's side won, there followed a rainy year with plenty of food. When Sun's side was the winner, the earth grew hot and dry and the losers had to pay in human lives. Whenever they lost, Sky Coyote and Morning Star tried to pay their debt with old people, whose time on earth was nearly finished anyway. But once in a while Sun insisted on having a young person.

How Rattlesnake Had His Revenge

The Luiseño Indians, who lived in the area north of what is now San Diego, also knew many constellations. Luiseño parents used to teach their children about the constellations by having them trace the patterns in the hearth with the sparks of live coals. Like the Chumash, the Luiseño thought of many of the bright stars as sky beings. They believed the North Star to be a great chief whose people moved in a circle around him. During ceremonies, the Luiseño danced around the sacred fire to imitate the circular motions of the stars.

Near the North Star is a constellation that they thought of as his heart and hand. This pattern is composed of stars you can see only when the sky is very clear and free of haze. As the following story explains, North Star lost one of his fingers when Rattlesnake bit it off.

When all the First People lived at Temecula in southern California, Rattlesnake lived there too. Everyone made fun of him because he was the only one with no arms or legs. North Star especially abused the poor fellow by throwing dirt at him and pulling him here and there by his hair. That made Rattlesnake very sad and angry.

One day Rattlesnake became particularly angry at North Star. He resolved to get even and took his case to Mother Earth.

Mother Earth considered the problem carefully before taking any action. Rattlesnake was angry and wanted revenge. That was not right, but he did have a right to protect himself. Mother Earth gave Rattlesnake two sharp-pointed sticks for protection. She also gave him the gift of poison. Rattlesnake was skeptical but decided to try his gift.

The next day North Star tormented Rattlesnake cruelly. Rattlesnake warned him but North Star just laughed. Then, using his new fangs, Rattlesnake bit off one of North Star's fingers.

Mother Earth decided to strengthen Rattlesnake's poison by providing three scorching days to hasten its action. When three very hot days come in a row, remember this story. Someone has just been bitten by Rattlesnake, and Mother Earth is making the bite more effective. If you doubt this story, look carefully at the hand of North Star on the next very clear night. You will see that one of his fingers is missing — bitten off by Rattlesnake.

The Seven Boys-Turned-Geese

Near the Star That Never Moves is the Big Dipper, which the Chumash thought of as seven young boys who had turned into geese. After being mistreated by their mothers, they went off on their own and eventually flew north. The following story contains a strong moral, which was echoed in the leader's speech during the important Chumash harvest ceremony called Hutash: "You, the elders, must show your children that you haven't forgotten them. Teach your children not to forget you." Though the boys in the story are treated badly by their mothers and fathers, they are always polite to each other and to their friend Raccoon. They act properly even though their parents do not. This is what happened when seven boys went hungry.

A very long time ago, when the world was young, animals were people. One day, early in the morning, a young boy's stepfather went out duck hunting. He did well, as usual, brought his catch home, and roasted plenty for supper. In those days the men did the cooking.

The mother and stepfather shared the ducks but didn't give any to the young boy. He watched them sadly as they ate. After supper, the mother told her son, "If you are hungry, go find your father and ask him for something to eat."

The little boy became very angry at this. His father had left them and now had another family of his own. The boy knew his father would probably not want to feed another child. Since his stepfather would give him nothing to eat, the boy decided to find his own food. So off he went.

He dug some roots and picked a few fresh green herbs and nibbled hungrily on them. Before long he found some edible bulbs called cacomites and ate them too. They filled him up.

Then he went home. Early in the afternoon his mother chased him away from the hut. Hurt and angry, he went out to his secret place. It was far away, where he could play alone and not be bothered by the noises of the camp. He finally got tired of playing and went to sleep.

When he awoke, it was already morning and he was hungry. He remembered the cacomites and how they had filled him up. He went out to dig some more for breakfast. While he was digging, another boy came along. He, too, had been chased away from his home and was hungry. The first boy taught the second boy how to dig for the bulbs, how to clean them, and how to cut and eat them. They had a great day together and spent the night at the secret hideaway.

When morning came, the boys got busy hunting and digging cacomites and roots to eat. Soon old Raccoon came along. He watched them for a short time and asked, "What are you doing?"

"We are digging roots and cacomites for our breakfast, Uncle," they replied courteously.

"Don't you have mothers and fathers to take care of you?" Raccoon asked.

"Yes," said one of them.

"But they don't want us anymore," added the other. "They chased us away from camp."

"Poor lonely, unfortunate boys!" exclaimed Raccoon. "I will take care of you. Follow me. I know where we can find more food." He led them to a place where a vegetable much like a potato grew. They began to dig for this tuber. A third boy came along and they all began to eat.

While they were eating, two more lonely boys came along. When they saw Raccoon and the three other boys, they asked politely, "May we join you?"

"Of course," Raccoon replied. "But there won't be enough food here. Follow me and I will take you to a place where you will all have plenty to eat." The five boys began digging and soon had enough for a big supper. Then Raccoon built a fire to keep them warm.

"Do you want to stay with me for the night?" Raccoon asked the five.

"Yes, oh, yes!" they exclaimed in unison.

Early the next morning, Raccoon asked the boys, "Shouldn't you go on home for breakfast?"

"Oh, no," they replied. "We like it with you. You take good care of us."

Raccoon then led them to a spot where there were roots, berries, and tubers in great abundance. While the five boys were digging, two more boys arrived. They, too, had been abandoned. They were invited for breakfast.

After a while, the oldest boy said, "I am going to travel north. Do you want to come with me?"

"Yes, we'd like to go too," the six other boys quickly responded.

"What about Uncle Raccoon?" asked one. "We don't want to leave him."

"He can come with us," said the oldest.

One boy had found some goose down. Gathering it all together, he placed a little on the head and shoulders of each boy.

"We're too much for you to take care of, Uncle Raccoon," said the boys. "Since our mothers have sent us away, we're really going to leave. Why don't you come along?"

"Very well, boys, I will come with you," said Raccoon, for he had grown quite fond of them. The boys put goose down on him too.

Then the oldest boy said, "Let's sing a special song." He began to lead them in a magic song to make them lighter. The boys slowly began to rise and move toward the sweatlodge. Because Raccoon couldn't fly, he had to follow on the ground.

The boys kept on singing all that night. In the morning, Raccoon took them to find breakfast. Soon, though, they resumed singing. Again they began to rise and circle the sweatlodge. They put goose down on Raccoon, but he still could not fly. They felt sad. Raccoon was sad too.

After breakfast the next morning, the boys told Raccoon that they could not wait for him any longer. They had to leave tomorrow. Everyone cried.

"Let's try one more time," begged one boy, "to make Raccoon fly."

They covered Raccoon completely in the magic down. He looked like a big white puffball with big black eyes, pointed ears, and a striped tail. How funny he looked! But he still couldn't fly.

Now every time the boys went out flying, they went higher and higher and had more trouble coming back to Raccoon in camp. One day the oldest boy cried out to Raccoon below. An old neighbor woman recognized his voice and ran to the boys' mothers. "How heartless you are! Come and see what has happened to your sons," she yelled.

"Come back, little son," one mother shouted angrily. "Come down here this very minute." But the boys only flew higher. By this time the mothers were all crying, and so was Raccoon.

Soon all the boys changed into wild geese. When they talked, it sounded like babies crying. Geese still sound that way today. Listen carefully the next time you see geese flying overhead. Listen and remember this story.

The boys-turned-geese kept rising higher until they came to Sky Country. They settled in the north and became the Big Dipper. The mothers are still looking for their boys. The mothers became the seven stars of the Pleiades, which rise in the northeast, ride high in the winter sky, and set in the northwest.

Eight Wise Men

The Chumash watched the Pleiades for calendar information, as did many other California tribes. They and their neighbors also told stories about this little bunch of stars. The only surviving Chumash tale about the Pleiades is a fragment that tells about seven men. A Chumash man named Fernando Librado learned it from his grandfather.

Librado later heard another version from a Chumash friend, which described the Pleiades as seven women. Anthropologist Travis Hudson, who studied Chumash astronomy, believed that the Chumash constellation represented women, probably the mothers of the boys who turned into geese, and that, as sometimes happens, Librado's grandfather got the story mixed up.

Dr. Hudson was puzzled by the meaning of this story, in which a star disappears, but then he learned from astronomers that one of the stars in the Pleiades was once much brighter. Over the centuries it has grown fainter, making it extremely difficult to see. He has suggested that this story explains the growing dimness of that star. If true, this indicates that the Chumash not only watched the skies very carefully, but passed down their knowledge from century to century.

At one time, eight wise men agreed that they should live together. They decided that if they pooled their knowledge and their skills, they would live far better than if each tried to live alone, for some were better at catching fish and others were better at reading the sky for weather and for signs to guide their lives. One of the men was skilled at finding the best nuts and berries, and another was expert at trapping small animals and making clothes from their hides.

Their partnership was going very well, but one day a wise man disappeared and no one knew where he had gone or what had become of him. Later, an old woman came by and asked, "Where is the eighth man? The last time I visited here there were eight of you."

They answered, "We do not know. One day we looked around and one of us had just disappeared. We haven't seen him since."

After telling Fernando Librado this story, his grandfather turned to the sky and pointed, saying, "Those stars there in the distance, the ones that came from the east, they are the men in my story. Not everyone will be able to go there."

The Seven Sisters

For the Luiseño, the Pleiades represent seven young sisters. Consistent with his behavior in other stories, Coyote acts very foolish in this one but also creates a constellation by forcing the seven sisters to retreat to the sky to escape his amorous intentions.

In the days of the myths, when the people went up to the sky to escape death, seven sisters climbed a rope that had been let down for them. When they had climbed partway to the sky, Coyote took hold of the rope and began to follow them. "I'll just come along. As you have no other man, I can be your husband."

The girls were horrified to think that Coyote wanted to be their husband, but they said nothing to him. The eldest cautioned, "Just keep going and don't encourage him. When we reach the sky, I have a plan to get rid of him."

The girls kept on climbing. Since they didn't say no to him, Coyote followed. Then, as soon as the girls reached the sky, the eldest took the flint knife she always carried and reached out to cut the rope. When Coyote saw what she was going to do, he tried to climb faster, but to no avail. The knife's sharp edge reached the rope before he could manage more than a few steps. Coyote fell away from the girls, but he stayed in the sky and became Aldebaran, the bright star that always follows the seven sisters.

The Wolf and the Crane

Several days after the Pleiades make their first appearance in the northeastern sky in early summer, the constellation Orion rises in the early morning to the south of the Pleiades. The spectacular pattern of three bright stars in a row which modern astronomers call the belt of the hunter Orion was often used by American Indians to time their ceremonies. The Chumash called it simply Three in a Row. No Chumash legends of Three in a Row have survived, but their neighbors told a variety of stories about these striking stars.

The Tachi Yokuts, who lived to the northeast of the Chumash, thought of the stars as a bear chasing an antelope. In another version, the Tachi Yokuts tell about a wolf and a crane rather than a bear. Using this story, the tribe taught that it is not good to be selfish.

Wolf was a good hunter, but he was also selfish. He went out hunting every day, but he brought nothing back for his wife, Crane, and their two boys. Wolf's family had a hard time finding enough to eat without his help.

One day when Wolf was hunting, Crane ran off with her two boys, hoping to find a better place to live. When Wolf returned home and discovered that Crane and his sons were gone, he became enraged. He decided to follow them and kill them. Because he had a good nose for tracking game, he soon picked up their scent and was on their trail.

Wolf was a fast runner, and soon he could see Crane and the boys before him. He tried to shoot her with his bow and arrow but she was flying too high. He followed his wife until she had to come down to rest. Then he shot her. When he walked over to where she lay and pushed her with his paw to see if she was still alive, she revived enough to impale him with her long, sharp bill. Though he fended her off and tried to pierce her with an arrow, she was able to knock him down and stab him until he was dead.

With only a quick look back at Wolf, Crane and her boys flew off. They flew high into the sky until they turned into stars. Crane is in front and the boys are following her — they are the three stars of Orion's belt.

Journey of the Piñon Gatherers

Most Native American groups recognized the Milky Way as special. For the Chumash it symbolized many things. Their common name for it was a long word that means Journey of the Piñon Gatherers, because both the Milky Way and the inside of piñon nuts are white. In the late fall and early winter, the Milky Way symbolized the northward journey the Chumash made to gather ripe piñon nuts. The part of the Milky Way that is near the constellation Cygnus splits and appears to follow two paths, which in winter are just visible on the western horizon after sunset. The Milky Way's appearance reminded the Chumash that it was also the pathway of the spirits of the dead. Since the Milky Way stretched completely around the earth, the Chumash also considered it to be a circular cord of feathers, just like the goose down that helped the boys who were abandoned by their mothers to fly north.

CALIFORNIA INDIAN STARS AND STAR PATTERNS

Star or constellation	*Western equivalent*	*Tribe*
Road of the Dead	Milky Way	Gabrielino
Journey of the Piñon Gatherers	Milky Way	Chumash
Star That Never Moves (Sky Coyote)	North Star	Chumash
Eight Wise Men	Pleiades	Chumash
Three in a Row	Orion's belt	Chumash
Morning Star	Unknown	Chumash
Seven Boys-Turned-Geese	Big Dipper	Chumash
Seven Sisters	Pleiades	Luiseño
Coyote	Aldebaran	Luiseño
Crane and Her Sons	Orion's belt	Tachi Yokuts

CHAPTER SEVEN

Chinook Wind

Stories from the Northwest Coast

A land of precipitous cliffs, rolling ocean surf, and mighty rivers, the Northwest Coast is the home of numerous sea-loving Indian tribes. Thick, dense greens, earthy browns, and deep sea blues are the colors of the landscape. Days of fog and rain are common, punctuated by brilliant blue skies when the weather clears. The entire area is dominated and divided by mountains. To the west are the Pacific Ocean, Puget Sound, and the Olympic Mountains. To the east and south are the woodlands, rivers, and streams of the Cascades and other mountain ranges.

The ancestors of the Native American peoples who live in the Northwest harvested the area's rich resources and built a complex culture that amazed the first European and Russian visitors. From the ocean these tribes caught seven different species of salmon. In the thick forests that come right down to the water's edge, they hunted bear, deer, and elk. Cedar, pine, and fir provided material for their graceful water craft, their sturdy houses, and their beautiful carvings.

Most of the tribes were highly conscious of social standing and had a ruling class that strived to amass as much wealth as possible. The Kwakiutl, who still live along the coast above Vancouver Island in Canada, developed the custom of putting on elaborate public feasts called potlatches in which the aristocrats demonstrated prosperity and power by bestowing valuable gifts on their guests. They and other coastal tribes carved beautiful masks for their colorful winter ceremonies. The Tlingit, the Haida, and other groups carved the imposing totem poles that have come to symbolize the Northwest peoples. Such totems, whether freestanding or part of a structure, were memorials to ancestors and depicted the family's mythical and true lineage.

Judging from the stories told by these peoples, magical, supernatural beings inhabited their forests and enlivened their winter evenings. For the coastal tribes, Raven the

trickster was an important figure. It was Raven who stole daylight from the sky god, who had kept it boxed up in his house in the sky, and then gave it to the people.

The customs of the inland tribes of the Plateau were closely related to those of the Plains Indians to the east. In their myths Coyote played a larger role. Their stories also revealed a strong sense of place; particular geographic features often appear in them. Some were creation stories that tell how mountains, valleys, or lakes were made.

The Elkskin

The Quileute lived on the northwestern tip of what is now the state of Washington, below Vancouver Island. They and their neighbors were skilled in using the products of the sea for food, clothing, and tools. They even did some whaling. Their dugout canoes were often quite long and featured handsome painted bows. The Quileute developed the special skill of capturing entire flocks of migrating ducks with huge nets on tall poles. The following Quileute story explains the origin of the constellation Cassiopeia, a well-defined stellar pattern that circles the North Star.

One bright autumn day, four brothers went elk hunting upriver in their canoe. The fifth and youngest brother did not go hunting that day but stayed home.

After they had gone a long way upriver, the eldest brother said, "This should be far enough."

"We should be able to find elk here!" said another enthusiastically.

Packing what they would need for lunch and for their hunting, the brothers set off on foot in search of elk.

Before they had traveled very far on the prairie, they saw a big man walking toward them. He greeted them and asked, "Where are you going?"

"We are elk hunting, Man of the Prairie," they replied.

"I know how you can find all the elk you want," he told them. "If you hide, I will drive elk down this ravine and you can kill them."

Now, this man was a very clever trickster. As he began to walk away, he looked back and told the brothers that he would trade their poor arrows for the good ones he had been saving. Since they were already in his power, they readily agreed. Soon they gave up their arrows for fine-looking but weak ones. The Man of the Prairie told them he was going off to find elk for the brothers.

Soon a big elk with huge antlers charged down the ravine toward the four brothers. Because their arrows were worthless, the elk was able to kill all four brothers. Then he turned himself back into the Man of the Prairie.

When his four older brothers did not return, the youngest brother went out looking for them. Before long, he found their empty canoe near the prairie. Like a good hunter, he followed his brothers' footsteps. Just as he came to the place where his brothers had met the big man, the Man of the Prairie came walking toward him.

The Man of the Prairie tried to trick the fifth brother just as he had the four others. The youngest brother, however, was a medicine man and had powerful magic of his own. The Man of the Prairie could not persuade the fifth brother to trade away his arrows; he was ready for such a trick. He could see how worthless the arrows were. "This must be how he fooled my brothers," he thought.

"I will not trade with you!" he shouted to the big man.

The Man of the Prairie turned to go away and the youngest brother hid behind a tree. Soon the man changed himself into a huge elk and came charging after the fifth brother just as he had charged the four brothers. But this one was ready with his bow. He shot four arrows — one for each

of his brothers — into the huge elk. Then he wrestled him to the ground and killed him. When he had skinned the elk, he stretched the skin and found it was even bigger than the prairie. He quickly threw the elkskin up into the sky.

And so it is there still, where you can see it on any clear night. Stars mark the holes where the fifth brother had driven in stakes while stretching the skin. Other stars are the elk's tail.

Coyote Loves a Star

The Klamath Indians lived along the head of the Klamath River in southeastern Oregon. Like their neighbors to the northwest, they placed a strong emphasis on acquiring wealth. Their winter houses, round earth lodges, and their summer shelters made of mats were like those of their eastern neighbors on the Plateau.

Like most Native American groups, the Klamath watched the stars to time their nightly ceremonies and to help define the yearly calendar. Storytellers used the stars as a nightly clock and knew when to complete their winter night's storytelling by noting the position of the three stars of Orion's belt. They thought of the bright twin stars Castor and Pollux as a boy and a girl who, when they appear above the eastern horizon in the early evenings of December, look down on Crater Lake and make it freeze. The bow belonging to these twin stars, which is probably a group of six stars in the eastern part of the constellation Gemini, rises somewhat before they do. The Klamath thought of the Pleiades as a group of little children, and they called the Big Dipper Ko'kinks —the divers. Ko'kinks is a group of loon-people who dive into the water one after another as they gamble to see who can dive the farthest out.

The Klamath had a rich store of myths and tales, many of which refer to the countryside. Nearly every major feature of the Klamath landscape — rocks, streams, and lakes — had its own legend and religious significance. Spirits, some of them frightening, lived everywhere. The following story, in which Coyote falls in love with an unnamed star, tells of the unplanned creation of Crater Lake by Coyote.

In the days when the world was new, Coyote was a cousin to humans and they lived and talked together. Coyote loved the night. He sat and gazed at the stars every chance he got. Before long, he began to notice one particularly bright, beautiful star. Coyote watched this star each night and talked to her for hours at a time. Soon he fell in love with her.

The more he talked to the lovely bright star, the more he loved her, and the more he wanted her to answer him. But she was silent night after night. She watched him far below as she slid across the black velvet of the sky on her nightly journey. He kept talking to her, but she remained silent.

This began to drive poor Coyote crazy! Every night he noticed that as she passed through the sky she almost touched a nearby mountain. That gave Coyote an idea.

Coyote decided to travel to that mountaintop. It was a long way, and he was extremely tired by the time he reached the place where she passed each night. He needed a rest but he was afraid to close his eyes — afraid he would miss his wonderful star. Coyote sat and waited for the sky to darken.

When she finally appeared, he realized his journey was worth it all. He almost fainted with joy when he saw his star close by. She was even more beautiful than he could ever have imagined as she danced across the sky with the other stars. Still Coyote waited. His heart was nearly jumping out of his mouth, but he said nothing.

Beautiful Star danced closer and closer to the very spot where he stood. He reached up with his paw to grab her hand but he could not quite touch her.

"Please reach down and take my hand so I can dance with you," he begged her.

She heard him and did as he asked. Beautiful Star lowered her lovely hand until she touched Coyote's paw. Then she drew him up and, slowly, they danced away from the mountaintop. They danced higher and higher until Coyote got very dizzy and grew afraid. It turned cold and quiet. None of the star people spoke. They just danced in starry silence.

Realizing he had made a terrible mistake, Coyote asked the stars to take him back to his home on earth. No one answered him. When they were at the very top of the sky and Coyote could no longer even see the distant mountaintop, Beautiful Star let go of his paw. Down, down he fell!

When Coyote hit the earth, he made a large hole and his blood, turned to water by the cold, filled the hole and created Crater Lake.

The next time you hear a coyote howling at the stars at night, you will remember this story and know that he is scolding Beautiful Star for letting go of him so suddenly.

Chinook Wind Wrestles Cold Wind

The grand Columbia River was a major passageway from the Plateau region east of the Cascade Mountains to the Pacific Ocean, first for the Native Americans of the region and later for the white settlers who moved into the area. Living upriver of the long series of rapids and steep channels that cut through the Cascades, on a region of the river called the Dalles, the Wasco Indians and their neighbors on the north banks of the Columbia, the Wishram, established themselves as traders with the many visitors who passed their way each year. From the Plateau region came buffalo robes, dried roots, and camas bulbs. From the coast and along the Columbia came salmon, canoes, marine shells, and shell beads.

Orion

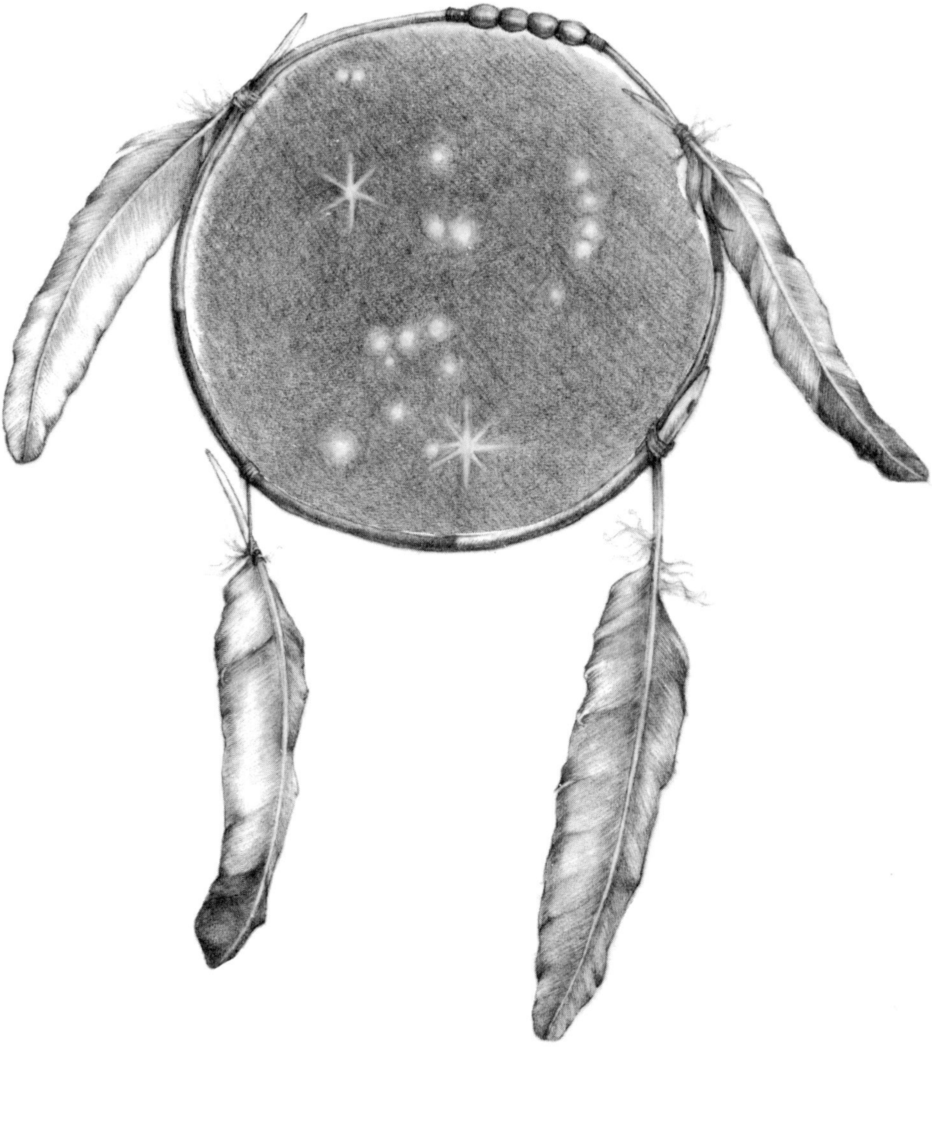

In the winter months, the wind brings with it the warmth of the Japanese current to the west, and it frees the snow-laden lower slopes of their winter burden. Because it comes from the direction of the Chinook tribe on the coast, the early traders called it the Chinook Wind. The Cold Wind comes from the direction of Walla Walla to the east. The struggle between Cold Wind and Chinook Wind is a theme that appears in several Wasco stories. As they looked up at the star pattern symbolizing the wrestling match during the nights when Cold Wind blew, the Wasco could take comfort that Chinook Wind would soon appear to overpower Cold Wind and unlock the ice-choked streams again. According to legend, this struggle began a long time ago when all stars were human beings.

Once there was an old grandfather who always caught many salmon in Big River. His grandson Chinook Wind was very proud of him. They always had plenty to eat and some to give away to more unfortunate fishermen's families. This began to change, however, when Chinook Wind left to visit relatives in a faraway camp. That was when Cold Wind decided he should take over.

Cold Wind wanted salmon too. But because he was lazy, he always came to Big River too late for good fishing. He would go down to the river to fish and see Chinook Wind's grandfather going home with plenty of salmon. Cold Wind usually caught nothing and this made him angry. He decided simply to take a salmon from Old Grandfather.

Of course, if he had been less impatient, he would not have had to steal the salmon. Old Grandfather was such a generous soul that he would gladly have given Cold Wind a share. But greedy people are seldom patient or courteous.

Every day, Cold Wind got up later and later. Every day he went down to fish too late to catch anything. Every day he stole a salmon from Old Grandfather. Oh, how bold he got!

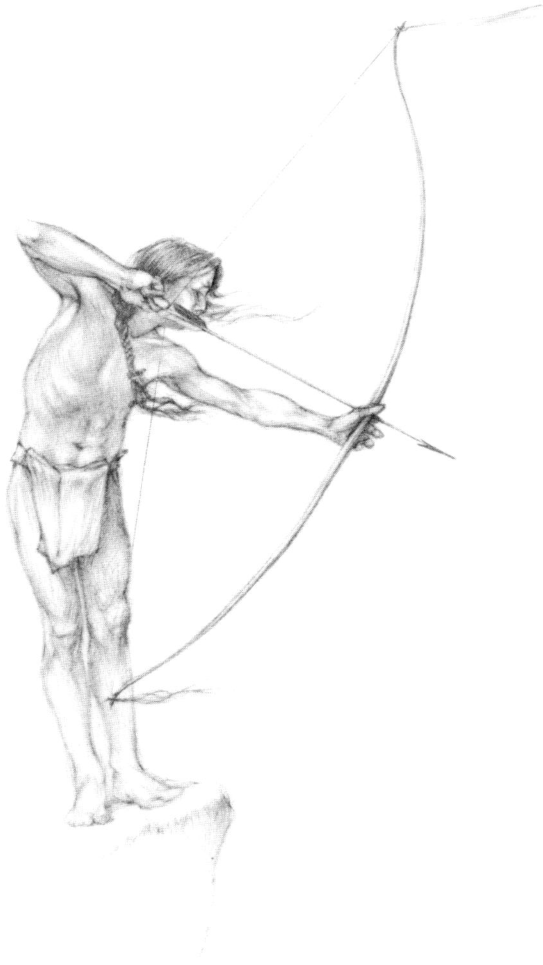

One day, Chinook Wind returned from his journey. When he heard how Cold Wind had been taking salmon from Old Grandfather, he grew angry and decided to teach him a lesson.

Chinook Wind hid in Old Grandfather's tipi and waited patiently until he came home from fishing. That day Old Grandfather returned whistling merrily, for he had caught more fish than usual. Everyone in the village would feast that night.

As usual, Cold Wind came roaring up to the tipi demanding salmon. This time, however, Chinook Wind boldly stepped out. "You cannot take any more of my grandfather's salmon!" he exclaimed.

"You cannot stop me, you scrawny boy," said Cold Wind. "I will wrestle you for Old Grandfather's salmon."

"All right," said Chinook Wind. "That is why I am come — to do whatever I have to do to protect the tribe and my grandfather."

And so the two wrestled. Chinook Wind fought hard and won the match. Because Chinook Wind won, Cold Wind can never again take salmon away from Old Grandfather. To this day Chinook Wind is stronger than Cold Wind.

If you look closely at the sky, you can see Chinook Wind and his brothers in their canoe close to Old Grandfather's salmon. Cold Wind and his brothers are in a canoe far behind. Cold Wind can never get Old Grandfather's last salmon.

NORTHWEST COAST INDIAN STARS AND STAR PATTERNS

Star or constellation	*Western equivalent*	*Tribe*
Elkskin	Cassiopeia	Quileute
Boy and Girl	Castor and Pollux	Klamath
Bow	Gemini	Klamath
Group of Children	Pleiades	Klamath
Ko'kinks (the Divers)	Big Dipper	Klamath
Chinook Wind Brothers	Orion's sword	Wasco
Cold Wind's Canoe	Orion's belt	Wasco

CHAPTER EIGHT

Star Beings

Tales from the Southeast

When the first European settlers arrived on the eastern shores of North America, they were astounded to encounter hundreds of different Indian groups and tribes, each with its own language, customs, and rituals. Each had its own myths that described the world and prescribed proper behavior. Many of the groups, particularly the smaller ones, were displaced or died of diseases such as smallpox and measles, which the settlers brought with them, before scholars could discover much about these tribes or their starlore. Most pioneers had little interest in Indian customs, since they regarded Native Americans as savages from whom they had little to learn.

The Cherokee, who are related to the Iroquois and who once lived in what is now eastern Tennessee and northern Georgia, were the largest tribe in the Southeast. Most of the Cherokee were forcibly removed from their eastern homelands to Oklahoma by the U.S. government in the early nineteenth century. Many died during the migration. In spite of this enormous disruption of their lives, much of

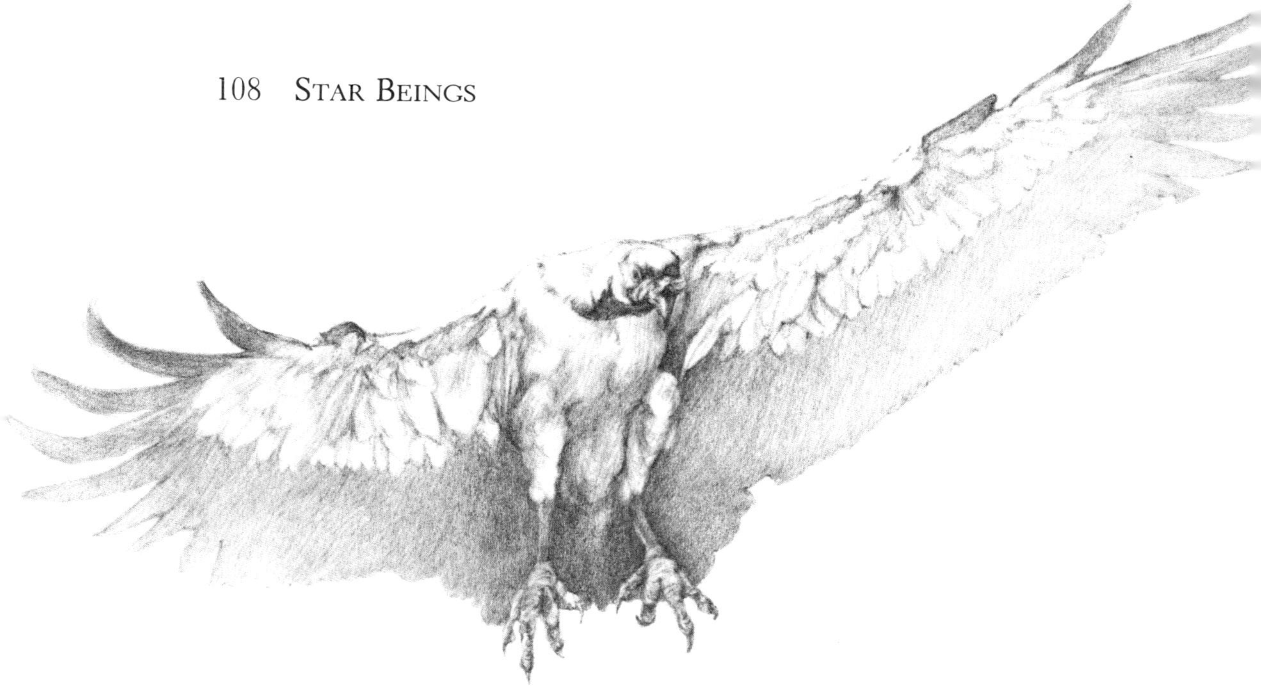

their folklore survived because, at the end of the nineteenth century, anthropologists from the Smithsonian Institution and elsewhere worked hard to compile and preserve it.

The Cherokee lived among the dense forests and clear streams of the Smoky Mountains, amid abundant deer, bear, rabbit, and other game animals. Their stories reflect their wooded, mountainous environment. According to their myths of creation, when the earth was still soft and unformed, the Great Buzzard caused the mountains to appear as he flew overhead. By the time he reached Cherokee country he was extremely tired and his wings kept hitting the ground. Each time his wings flopped down he created a valley, and when he raised them his wings made a mountain. All the other animals were afraid that the entire world would turn into mountains if he kept it up, so they called to him to stop, but the land of the Cherokee is nevertheless full of mountains.

The Door through the Sky

Many Native American tribes thought of the stars as bright lights against a vault of solid material. The Cherokee believed that the solid sky swung up and down continually. When the sky went up, there was an open place between it and the ground that acted as a door. This belief is illustrated by a story the Cherokee told about a visit to the sun, whom they thought of as a woman.

Once seven young men decided to travel to the sun. Off they walked, but after many days and many adventures, when they reached the sunrise place at the end of the earth, they discovered that the sky was solid. They could not get through to visit the sun. As they stood there, wondering what to do, the sky vault lifted, making a kind of doorway to the other side. Perhaps they could slip under to find the sun and see what her home was like.

Just then the sun herself appeared in the doorway and began to climb the sky. She was very bright and cast off so much heat that the young men had to step back and cover their eyes. One of the men decided to try the doorway. He leaped forward just as the sky closed again with a crash, crushing him between the sky and the earth. The remaining six decided it was too risky to try their luck, and, though they missed their friend, they turned back toward home. Somehow, the return took longer than the trip to the sun, and they were old men when they finally made it home again. They never did see the face of the sun.

What the Stars Are Like

The Cherokee held various beliefs about the stars. Some believed that the stars were great balls of light. Others said they were human beings who lived in Sky Country. In some circumstances, stars in animal form could be approached by humans. This story describes one such encounter, which helps explain the nature of stars.

Late one night a Cherokee hunting party sat around their mountain camp. They noticed two lights moving along near the top of a distant mountain ridge. They watched until the lights disappeared.

The next two nights they again watched the bright lights on the same mountain ridge. This was a wonder. No one had ever seen anything like it before. After discussing for some time what these lights could be, they decided to investigate.

The next morning they set out for the distant ridge. Arriving at the place, they searched and searched for the source of the lights. They saw no lights but, after looking for some time, they finally found two large, furry creatures about as big as two outstretched arms. The creatures had tiny heads and, when the wind blew, their fur parted to show downy feathers from which sparks flew.

The men were delighted with these strange beings and decided to take them back to camp. They kept them for several days and noticed how tame and docile the creatures were. Every night they shone bright like the stars. When daylight approached, they turned into dull balls of gray fur, except when a gust of wind stirred their feathers. Then their sparks flew.

None of the men thought the creatures might try to escape, so no one was prepared for what happened on the seventh night. As the men busied themselves with their tasks, the odd creatures began to rise from the ground. Soon they were bright, shining balls above the tops of the highest trees. Higher and higher they went until they were just two glowing spots in the night sky.

That is how the hunters knew they had captured two stars.

The Celestial Canoe

The Alabama Indians, who lived south of the Cherokee and were closely related to the Creek Indians, knew the North Star simply as the stationary star. The bowl of the Big Dipper, which rotates about it, they thought of as having the shape of a canoe. As this Celestial Canoe circles the North Star, it seems to touch the earth.

The Alabama and the Cherokee, as well as other Native American groups, watched the skies throughout the seasons and evolved legends to fit the patterns they observed. They knew that a story could educate listeners about the motion of the stars and entertain as well. In this tale, visitors from the sky ride a canoe down to the earth and get out to play ball, probably a game played with rackets something like lacrosse sticks. They have plenty of time, for at the latitude where the Alabama Indians lived, the bowl of the Big Dipper appears to touch the northwestern horizon at about 10 P.M. during the month of August. As the entire starry globe rotates, most of the Big Dipper disappears below the northern horizon for several hours. When the canoe reappears in the northeast, the sky people climb back in and ride it upward until dawn. Then they disappear from view in the light of the sun.

This same cycle occurs for several weeks before and after

the first week in August. For example, in July, the Celestial Canoe begins to set at about 11 P.M. and fully reappears just before dawn. In late September, when the stars of the Celestial Canoe become visible soon after dark, part of the canoe will have already set in the northwest.

Analyzing the myth in this way helps us understand another portion of the story. When the children and their father journey to the sky to find the mother, they meet an old woman who gives them squash to eat. However much they eat, there is always more. The Celestial Canoe disappears at night and then reappears in the early morning between July and September, the time when squash and other autumn harvest foods are plentiful. We suspect that the dance referred to in the story was the celestial counterpart of nightly dances held during the annual Alabama ceremony called the Busk. It was generally celebrated in late July when the first of the green corn became just ripe enough to eat. The Busk was a time of grand celebration for the coming plenteous harvest.

Finally, we can also suggest what the small canoe in the story represented. When the mother and children attempt to escape to the sky the second time, the mother is in the Celestial Canoe. She has placed her children in the second, small one. Although the father is unable to reach the large canoe, he is able to stop the small one. This suggests that the small canoe follows the Celestial Canoe into the sky. Looking at the night sky, the most obvious candidate is the handle of the Big Dipper. But more important, it follows the bowl of the Big Dipper through the sky. At the latitude where the Alabama Indians lived, the handle dips well below the horizon. By the time the small canoe has fully left the northern horizon, the Celestial Canoe is already well into the sky.

The story of the Celestial Canoe was a way for the Alabama elders to teach some simple astronomy to their children. It reminded everyone in the tribe that when the Celestial Canoe began to reach the northern horizon in the early evening, it would soon be time for the Busk.

Back in the days when stars were people, they could travel back and forth between the earth and sky. Some of these sky people regularly came down to earth in a canoe. While on earth, they played a ball game on a large, grassy field and then, when they were finished, they went back to their canoe, began singing, and rose to the sky. Every so often they would return to play ball in the same place.

One time, as the sky people played on earth, a man was hiding nearby, watching their game, spellbound. Suddenly the ball came right toward him and landed at his feet. Still entranced, he could not move. But when a beautiful sky woman ran after the ball, he leaped from his hiding place and grabbed her. Frightened by the man, the other players jumped in their canoe, started singing, and returned to the sky. The man took the beautiful woman home and married her. In time they had two children.

After several years the mother became homesick for the sky and soon devised a plan to return. She told her children to ask their father to go hunting and bring home meat to eat. He left for the nearby valley, but soon realized he had forgotten his skinning knife. He returned quickly — too soon for the mother and children to leave.

Again the mother instructed the children to ask for meat. This time she said, "Ask for deer that live on yonder mountain." Again they followed her instructions and their father set off to hunt.

Meanwhile, the mother and children climbed in the canoe, began to sing, and started to rise toward Sky Country. Their father returned in time to catch the canoe, pulling them back to earth.

In the weeks that followed, the woman made another canoe, a small one, and put it in a safe hiding place. Before long, her husband went out hunting again. The woman got in one canoe and put her children in the little one. She began singing and they all started to rise. The father again ran back, but this time he managed to stop only the little canoe with his children. The other canoe had flown too high. The mother kept singing and rising until she got to Sky Country.

The children missed their mother very much and begged their father to let them follow her. He gave in finally, and they all got in a canoe, sang, and began to rise just as she had.

The first person they came upon in Sky Country was an old crone. The father asked her, "Can you help my children find their mother?"

The old woman told him that his wife was dancing not far away. Then she cooked them dinner and they all sat down to eat. When the children saw the small pieces of squash the old woman served, they thought they could never eat their fill. Yet no sooner were their plates empty than more food magically appeared. Their plates were still full when they had all eaten as much as they could.

While they were resting, the old crone told them that their mother would return to her senses if they hit her with a corncob. She gave them each a piece of an old corncob and told them they could find their mother dancing at a neighbor's house.

The children and their father hurried to the house. The woman suddenly danced around them. The older child threw his piece of corncob but missed his mother. Again she danced near them. Both children missed. The last time she spun through the house, the younger child hit her skirt with his corncob.

Recognizing them at last, she cried with joy, "My children are here!" She ran up and gathered them to her in a big hug.

"Let us all go home," said her husband. And they all got in the canoe and came back to earth.

A long time after this, the mother and children again disappeared into the sky in the large canoe. When the father came back from his hunting trip he waited a couple of days for them to come home. When they did not return, he got in the small canoe and started singing. While he was traveling upward, he made the mistake of looking down. He tumbled out of the canoe and was killed when he fell to earth.

The woman and her children went home to join the people who still come down here to play ball on warm autumn nights.

Anitsutsa — The Boys

Like most Indian groups, the Cherokee told a story about the Pleiades. In this one, the boys play a game that was extremely popular among the Cherokee, the Alabama, the Creek, the Choctaw, and other tribes of the Southeast. The Cherokee called the game *gatayu'sti*, but early European settlers named it *chunky*, after the Creek Indian name for it. As in most Native American games, the players and the onlookers often gambled on the outcome. One player would roll a stone disk, about an inch thick and three inches in diameter, on a level grassy playing ground. The other players would hurl specially made poles, some as long as eight feet, toward it. The player whose stick came closest to the stone got one point. If the stick actually hit the stone, he earned two points. The following story seems to warn against becoming so involved in playing a game that everyday duties are forgotten.

Long ago there were seven boys. Boys were not much different then than now. They liked to play all day long. These seven particularly enjoyed playing *gatayu'sti*.

Mothers were not much different then either. The boys' mothers scolded them for playing all day and neglecting their chores. But the scolding did no good.

One day the mothers decided to teach their boys a lesson. They found some *gatayu'sti* stones and boiled them along with a tiny bit of corn for the boys' lunch. The boys had played hard and were hungry when they finally came home to eat. The mothers scooped the stones and corn into bowls, saying, "You seem to like playing with a stone more than helping in the cornfield. Have some stones with your lunch!"

Naturally the boys couldn't eat the soup. They became very angry at their mothers and resolved to run away so they could play all day long and not be bothered. And so they joined hands and began to dance. As they danced they sang a song, praying that the spirits would help them.

Before long, the mothers became worried and went looking for the boys. They went first to the open field where the boys played with their stone wheel. They found the boys there, dancing instead of playing *gatayu'sti.* As the mothers got closer, they noticed that the boys' feet didn't touch the ground. They were dancing on air, and they were rising fast.

Alarmed, the mothers ran toward the boys, shouting, "Come back, come back!"

But it was too late. By the time the mothers reached the place where the boys danced, they had risen overhead. One boy was a little lower than the rest. His mother was able to pull him down with one of the long curved poles the boys used for their wheel game.

The other six boys continued to rise, singing as they went. They took their place happily in Sky Country, where they are dancing still.

Where the Dog Ran

> The Cherokee thought of the Milky Way as a trail of cornmeal spread across the sky, which may be related to the fact that, in the Northern Hemisphere, the Milky Way is best seen in the summer and early fall, when the corn is ripening and ready to harvest. They called the Milky Way Where the Dog Ran.

In the south, some people used to grind corn with a corn mill. Each morning they would fill the mill with corn and grind it to a fine white meal. One morning, three women came to fill the mill and noticed a lot of the meal they had ground the day before was gone. They found some of the meal spread around, making a big mess on the ground.

"Who do you suppose stole our cornmeal?" asked one woman.

"Look at these tracks," another woman replied. "They tell the story!"

And, to be sure, the tracks revealed important clues about the culprit. They were dog tracks. A dog had stolen their meal and scattered some of it on the ground around the mill.

"What shall we do?" asked a third woman.

"Let us lie in wait for him tonight," said the woman who had found the tracks.

After their evening meal, the three women crouched down near the mill to watch for the thief. A short time after midnight they heard a rustling noise, and a dog from the north leaped into the clearing and ran straight to the corn mill. He began to eat, scattering meal everywhere in his haste.

The women sprang out of hiding and ran to the clearing, surrounding the dog. They whipped him and chased him back to the north, where he belonged. As he ran off, howling, the cornmeal spilled from his mouth and left a milky white trail behind him, which quickly spread across the sky.

SOUTHEAST INDIAN STARS AND STAR PATTERNS

Star or constellation	*Western equivalent*	*Tribe*
Celestial Canoe	Big Dipper (bowl)	Alabama
Small Celestial Canoe	Big Dipper (handle)	Alabama
Anitsutsa — The Boys	Pleiades	Cherokee
Where the Dog Ran	Milky Way	Cherokee

Glossary

Unless otherwise indicated, all constellation designations refer to Northern Hemisphere star patterns as they are defined by Middle Eastern and European tradition.

Alabama	Indian tribe that lived along the Alabama River; closely related to the Creek Indians
Alcor (al-KOR)	Faint companion to the star Mizar in the constellation Ursa Major; Alcor and Mizar look like a double star when seen with the naked eye
Aldebaran (al-DEB-a-ran)	Brightest star in the constellation Taurus
Algonquin (al-GONG-kin)	Tribe from the area near Ottawa, Canada
Anitsutsa (a-NI-tsu-tsa)	The Boys, Cherokee name for the Pleiades
Antares (an-TAR-eez)	Brightest star in the summer constellation Scorpius (the Scorpion)
Artemis (AR-te-mis)	Greek goddess of the hunt
Assiniboin (a-SIN-a-boyn)	Northern Plains Sioux tribe residing in southern Saskatchewan, Canada
Baakil (BA-a-kill)	Tachi Yokuts name for the flea in the story "Baakil and His Five Wives"
Canopus (ka-NO-pus)	Second-brightest star in the sky; brightest star in the Southern Hemisphere constellation Argo (the Ship *Argo*)
Capella (ka-PEL-a)	Brightest star in the constellation Auriga (the Charioteer)
Cassiopeia (KAS-ee-o-PEE-ya)	Constellation near the North Star (named for the Greek goddess Cassiopeia); a circumpolar constellation that is visible year-round from the Northern Hemisphere
Castor (KAS-ter)	Bright star in the constellation Gemini (the Twins)
Cayuga (kay-YOU-ga)	Tribe of the Iroquois Confederacy living in western New York State
Cherokee (CHER-uh-key)	Southeastern tribe that lived in South Carolina and Georgia; the U.S. government forced most of the tribe to move to Oklahoma in the mid-1800s

Cheyenne	(shy-ANN)	Northern Plains tribe of Algonquin stock living in eastern Wyoming and western Nebraska
Chinook	(shi-NOOK)	Northwest Coast tribe that inhabited the Columbia River valley; also the warm, moist southwest wind blowing inland from the sea in winter and spring
Choctaw	(CHOK-taw)	Southeastern tribe that lived in Louisiana and Mississippi
Chumash	(CHOO-mash)	Southern California tribe that lived in the area now occupied by the coastal city of Santa Barbara
Cochiti	(COACH-uh-tee)	Pueblo tribe living along the Rio Grande between Albuquerque and Santa Fe, New Mexico
Coeur d'Alene	(KERR da-LANE)	Tribe living in the Plateau area of northern Washington State
Corona Borealis	(kuh-ROW-na bow-ree-ALICE)	Early summer constellation (the Northern Crown)
Corvus	(KOR-vus)	Spring constellation (the Crow)
Cygnus	(SIG-nus)	Summer constellation (the Swan)
Dilyehe	(dil-YEH-heh)	Navajo name for the constellation Pleiades
Gabrielino	(GAY-bree-a-LEE-no)	Southern California tribe; neighbors of the Chumash
gatayu'sti	(ga-tay-YOU-sti)	Cherokee name for game popular among the southeastern tribes played with a stone disk and pole; settlers called the game *chunky*
Gemini	(JEM-i-nye)	Winter constellation (the Twins)
Haida	(HIGH-da)	Tribe living along the coast of British Columbia, Canada
hogan	(HO-gan)	Traditional Navajo winter dwelling, oriented so the doorway opens toward the east
Hopi	(HOE-pee)	Pueblo tribe living in northern Arizona
Hutash	(WHO-tash)	Chumash name for the earth; also the name of a ceremony held to celebrate the harvest and honor the earth
Iroquois	(EAR-uh-kwoi)	Confederacy of tribes that lived in western and northern New York, consisting originally of the Mohawk, Oneida, Onondaga, Cayuga, and Seneca groups

Kiowa	(KAI-uh-wah)	Southwestern Plains tribe living in western Oklahoma and northern Texas
Klamath	(KLA-meth)	Tribe that lived in the heavily forested areas of northeastern California and southern Oregon
Ko'kinks	(KO-kinks)	Klamath name for Big Dipper
Kotcimanyako	(KOT-si-man-YAK-O)	Name of the mythical Cochiti Pueblo girl who scattered the stars
Kwakiutl	(KWA-key-you-dle)	Northwest Coast tribe living on the islands of western British Columbia, Canada
Luiseño	(loowi-SAY-nyo)	Southern California coastal tribe; southern neighbors of the Chumash
Mandan	(MAN-dan)	Western Plains Sioux tribe residing in North Dakota
Micmac	(MIK-mak)	Tribe residing in the Maritime Provinces of Canada
Mohawk	(MOW-hawk)	Western New York State tribe; a member of the Iroquois Confederacy
Monache	(MO-na-che)	Name for a group of six small, independent central California tribes living near Kings River
Mono	(MOW-no)	One of the central California Monache tribes
Navajo	(NAV-a-ho)	Southwestern tribe living in northeastern Arizona, western New Mexico, and southern Utah; the largest North American tribe
Nez Perce	(nez PURSE)	Plateau tribe that lived in Idaho and western Montana
Oneida	(oh-NYE-da)	Tribe residing in western New York State; a member of the Iroquois Confederacy
Onondaga	(ah-nen-DAW-ga)	Tribe from upper New York State; a member of the Iroquois Confederacy
Oot-kwa-tah	(oot-KWA-tah)	Onondaga term for the Pleiades; a band of dancing children
Orion	(oh-RYE-on)	Winter constellation (the Hunter)
Osage	(OH-sage)	A Plains tribe that lived in southern Missouri
Pawnee	(paw-NEE)	A Plains tribe that lived in central Nebraska
peon	(PEA-on)	Chumash gambling game

Picuris	(pic-ur-EESE)	Pueblo tribe living in northern New Mexico
Pitahawirata	(pita-HA-wir-ah-tah)	One of the Pawnee South Bands
Pleiades	(PLEE-a-deez)	Star cluster in the fall and winter constellation Taurus
Pleione	(PLY-oh-nee)	Bright star in the Pleiades
Polaris	(po-LA-ris)	The North Star
Pollux	(POL-uks)	Bright star in the constellation Gemini
Pueblo	(PWEB-low)	Tribes living along the Rio Grande in New Mexico, western New Mexico (Zuni), and northern Arizona (Hopi)
Quileute	(KWIL-a-yute)	A Northwest Coast tribe that lived on the western coast of Washington State
Rio Grande	(REE-oh GRAND)	River originating in southern Colorado that passes through New Mexico and Texas and empties into the Gulf of Mexico. It forms the southeastern boundary between Texas and Mexico. The Rio Grande Valley was an important trading route in prehistoric times.
Scorpius	(SKOR-pee-us)	Summer constellation (the Scorpion)
Seneca	(SEN-eh-ka)	Westernmost of the Iroquois tribes, from western New York State
Shasta	(SHAS-ta)	Tribe that lived in southwestern Oregon and northern California, south of the Klamath Indians
Sirius	(SIR-ee-us)	Brightest star in the sky, located in the constellation Canis Major (the Great Dog). Sirius is often called the Dog Star because it follows Orion across the sky.
Skidi	(SKEE-dee)	Wolf Band of the Pawnee Indians. The Skidi had a well-developed lore of the stars.
Snohomish	(snow-HO-mish)	Tribe that once lived on the east coast of Puget Sound near the town of Everett, Washington
Tachi Yokuts	(TA-chee YO-kuts)	A band of the Yokuts Indians of south-central California
Tapirapé	(TA-pa-RA-pay)	Tribe of Indians living in the Amazon rain forest

Taurus	(TOR-us)	Fall and winter constellation (the Bull)
Tirawahat	(TIR-a-wa-hut)	Pawnee supreme spirit
Tlingit	(TLING-it)	Tribe living on the islands of northwestern British Columbia, Canada
travois	(treh-VWAH)	A device used for carrying loads behind a dog or a horse which consisted of a net attached to two poles
Ursa Major	(ERR-sa MAY-jer)	Circumpolar constellation (the Great Bear, or Big Dipper)
Vega	(VEE-ga)	Bright star in the constellation Cygnus (the Swan)
Wasco	(WA-skoh)	Northwest Coast Indian tribe that lived along the Columbia River in southern Washington State, south of the Wishram
Wishram	(WISH-ram)	Northwest Coast Indian tribe that lived along the Columbia River in southern Washington State
Zeus	(zooss)	The supreme deity of the ancient Greeks
Zuni	(ZOO-nee)	Pueblo Indian tribe living in western New Mexico

Suggested Further Reading

Bierhorst, John. *The Ring in the Prairie: Legends of the American Indian.* New York: Dial Press, 1970.

Bierhorst, John. *The Whistling Skeleton.* New York: Four Winds Press, 1982.

Bierhorst, John. *The Sacred Path.* New York: Morrow, 1983.

Bierhorst, John. *The Hungry Woman.* New York: Morrow, 1984.

Bierhorst, John. *The Mythology of North America.* New York: Morrow, 1985.

Clark, Ella E. *Indian Legends of the Pacific Northwest.* Berkeley: University of California Press, 1953.

Clark, Ella E. *Indian Legends from the Northern Rockies.* Norman: University of Oklahoma Press, 1966.

Curtis, Edward S. *The Girl Who Married a Ghost and Other Tales from the North American Indian.* New York: Four Winds Press, 1978.

Curtis, Natalie. *The Indians' Book.* New York: Dover Publications, 1968.

Cushing, Frank H. *Zuni Folk Tales.* Tucson: University of Arizona Press, 1986.

Erdoes, Richard, and Alfonso Ortiz, eds. *American Indian Myths and Legends.* New York: Pantheon Books, 1984.

Feldman, Susan, ed. *The Story-Telling Stone: Myths and Tales of the American Indians.* New York: Dell Publishing Co., 1965.

Fisher, Anne B. *Stories California Indians Told.* Berkeley: Parnassus Press, 1957.

Grinnell, George B. *By Cheyenne Campfires.* Lincoln: University of Nebraska Press, 1926.

Hayes, Joe. *Coyote &.* Santa Fe, N.M.: Mariposa Publishing, 1983.

Kroeber, Theodora. *The Inland Whale.* Berkeley: University of California Press, 1959.

Marriott, Alice Lee. *Winter-telling Stories.* New York: Crowell, 1969.

Marriott, Alice Lee. *Dance around the Sun.* New York: Crowell, 1977.

Marriott, Alice, and Carol K. Rachlin. *American Indian Mythology.* New York: Crowell, 1968.

Marriott, Alice, and Carol K. Rachlin. *Plains Indian Mythology.* New York: Crowell, 1975.

Mullet, G. M. *Spider Woman Stories.* Tucson: University of Arizona Press, 1979.

Ramsey, Jarold. *Coyote Was Going There.* Seattle and London: University of Washington Press, 1977.

Rose, Anne K. *Spider in the Sky.* New York: Harper & Row, 1978.

Thompson, Stith. *Tales of the North American Indians.* Bloomington and London: University of Indiana Press, 1966.

Turner, Frederick W., III, ed. *The Portable North American Indian Reader.* New York: Viking Press, 1973.

Williamson, Ray. *Living the Sky: The Cosmos of the American Indian.* Boston: Houghton Mifflin, 1984.

Wood, C.E.S. *A Book of Indian Tales.* New York: Vanguard, 1929.

Bibliography

Epigraph

Gibbon, William B. "Asiatic Parallels in North American Starlore." *Journal of American Folklore* 85 (1972): 236–47.

Seven Dancing Stars: Legends of the Pleiades

Beauchamp, William M. "Onondaga Tale of the Pleiades." *Journal of American Folklore* 13 (1900): 281. Gifford, Edward W., and Gwendoline H. Block. *California Indian Nights Entertainments.* Glendale, Calif.: A. H. Clark Co., 1930, p. 226. Gayton, Anna H., and Stanley S. Newman. "Yokuts and Western Mono Myths." *University of California Anthropological Records* 5, no. 1 (1948): 26, 50. Kroeber, A. L. "Myths of South Central California." *University of California Publications in American Archaeology and Ethnology* 4, no. 4 (1907): 213–14.

The Celestial Bear: Stories of the Big Dipper

Hagar, Stansbury. "The Celestial Bear." *Journal of American Folklore* 13 (1900): 92–103. Teit, James. "The Salishan Tribes of the Western Plateaus." *Smithsonian Institution Bureau of American Ethnology* 45 (1939): 178–79. McWhorter, Lucullus. "Legend of the Great Dipper and the Big White Road across the Sky." Folder 2 in the L. V. McWhorter Archives, Holland Library, State University of Washington Manuscript Collection, Exhibit 8. Quoted in Ella E. Clark, *Indian Legends of the Pacific Northwest.* Berkeley: University of California Press, 1953, pp. 152–55. Shelton, William. *The Story of the Totem Pole.* Everett, Washington: Kane and Marcus, 1935.

Coyote Scatters the Stars: Myths from the Southwest

Haile, Berard F. *Starlore Among the Navaho.* Santa Fe, N.M.: Museum of Navajo Ceremonial Art, 1946, p. 4. Parsons, Elsie C. "Tales of the Cochiti Indians." *Smithsonian Institution Bureau of American Ethnology Bulletin* 98 (1931): 4. Parsons, Elsie C. "Tales of the Cochiti Indians." *Smithsonian Institution Bureau of American Ethnology Bulletin* 98 (1931): 4. Harrington, John P., and H. H. Roberts. "Picuris Children's Stories." *Smithsonian Institution Bureau of American Ethnology Annual Reports* 43 (1928): 289–447.

General Information: Brewer, Sallie P. "Notes on Navaho Astronomy." In *For the Dean: Essays in Anthropology in Honor of Byron Cummings.* Tucson: University of Arizona Press, 1950, pp. 133–36. Franciscan Fathers. *An Ethnologic Dictionary of the Navaho Language.* St. Michaels, Ariz.: St. Michaels Mission, 1910. O'Bryan, Aileen. "The Diné: Origin Myths of the Navaho Indians." *Smithsonian Institution Bureau of American Ethnology Bulletin* 16 (1956).

When Stars Fell to Earth: Legends of the Pawnee

Murie, James R. "Stone God." Dorsey Manuscript File, Field Museum, Chicago, n.d. Quoted in Von Del Chamberlain, *When Stars Came Down to Earth.* Los Altos, Calif.: Ballena Press, 1982, pp. 147–49. Dorsey, George. "The Pawnee: Mythology." *Carnegie Institution of Washington Publications* 59 (1906): 119–22. Dorsey, George. "The Pawnee: Mythology." *Carnegie Institution of Washington Publications* 59 (1906): 233–36. Murie, James R. "Ceremonies of the Pawnee," edited by Douglas Parks. *Smithsonian Contributions to Anthropology* 27 (1981): 362.

General Information: Chamberlain, Von Del. *When Stars Came Down to Earth.* Los Altos, Calif.: Ballena Press, 1982. Weltfish, Gene. *The Lost Universe.* Lincoln: University of Nebraska Press, 1977.

Morning Star: Legends of the Plains Indians

Wissler, Clark, and D. C. Duvall. "Blackfoot Mythology." *American Museum of Natural History, Anthropological Papers* 2 (1908): 58–61. Fletcher, Alice C., and Francis La Flesche. "The Omaha Tribe." *Bureau of American Ethnology Annual Report* 27 (1905–1906) *17*: 223–60. Dorsey, George. "The Arapahoe Sun Dance." *Field Columbian Museum Anthropological Papers* 4 (1903): 191–228. Lowie, Robert H. "The Assiniboine." *American Museum of Natural History, Anthropological Papers* 4 (1909): 117.

General Information: Ewers, John C. *The Blackfeet: Raiders on the Northwestern Plains.* Norman: University of Oklahoma Press, 1958. Lowie, Robert H. *Indians of the Plains.* Lincoln: University of Nebraska Press, 1982.

They Live in the Sky: Stories of the California Indians

Heizer, Robert. "The Indians of Los Angeles County: Hugo Reid's Letters of 1852." *Southwest Museum Papers* 21 (Highland Park, Calif., 1968): 65–68. Hudson, Travis, and Ernest Underhay. *Crystals in the Sky: An Intellectual Odyssey Involving Chumash Astronomy, Cosmology, and Rock Art.* Socorro, N.M.: Ballena Press, 1978. DuBois, Constance G. "Mythology of the Mission Indians." *Journal of American Folklore* 19 (1906): 52–60. Blackburn, Thomas. *December's Child: A Book of Chumash Oral Narratives.* Berkeley and Los Angeles: University of California Press, 1975. Hudson, Travis, Thomas Blackburn, Rosario Curletti, and Janice Timbrook. *The Eye of the Flute: Chumash Traditional History and Ritual as Told by Fernando Librado Kitsepawit to John P. Harrington.* Santa Barbara: Santa Barbara Museum of Natural History, 1977, pp. 35–36. DuBois, Constance Goddard. "The Religion of the Luiseño Indians of Southern California." *University of California Publications in American Archaeology and Ethnology* 8 (1908): 164. Kroeber, A. L. "Myths of South Central California." *University of California Publications in American Archaeology and Ethnology* 4 (1904): 214.

General Information: Blackburn, Thomas. *December's Child: A Book of Chumash Oral Narratives.* Berkeley and Los Angeles: University of California Press, 1975, pp. 245–50. Hudson, Travis, and Ernest Underhay. *Crystals in the Sky: An Intellectual Odyssey Involving Chumash Astronomy, Cosmology, and Rock Art.* Socorro, N.M.: Ballena Press, 1978.

Chinook Wind: Stories from the Northwest Coast

Reagan, Albert, and L.V.W. Walters. "Tales from the Hoh and Quileute." *Journal of American Folklore* 46 (1933): 326–27. Wood, C.E.S. *A Book of Indian Tales.* New York: Vanguard, 1929, pp. 97–99. McWhorter, Lucullus. "Orion." Folder 3 in the L. V. McWhorter Archives, Holland Library, State University of Washington Manuscript Collection, Exhibit 8. Quoted in Ella E. Clark, *Indian Legends of the Pacific Northwest.* Berkeley: University of California Press, 1953, p. 157.

Star Beings: Tales from the Southeast

Mooney, James. "The Myths of the Cherokee." *Bureau of American Ethnology Annual Report* 19 (1900): 255–56. Mooney, James. "The Myths of the Cherokee." *Bureau of American Ethnology Annual Report* 19 (1900): 257. Swanton, John R. "Myths of the Southeastern Indians." *Bureau of American Ethnology Bulletin* 88 (1929): 138–39. Mooney, James. "The Myths of the Cherokee." *Bureau of American Ethnology Annual Report* 19 (1900): 258. Mooney, James. "The Myths of the Cherokee." *Bureau of American Ethnology Annual Report* 19 (1900): 259.

General Information: Hagar, Stansbury. "Cherokee Star-Lore." In *Anthropological Papers Written in Honour of Franz Boas.* New York: G. E. Stechert and Co., 1906, pp. 354–66. Mooney, James. "The Myths of the Cherokee." *Bureau of American Ethnology Annual Report* 19 (1900): 3–548. Swanton, John R. "Myths of the Southeastern Indians." *Bureau of American Ethnology Bulletin* 88 (1929): 1–275. Swanton, John R. "Religious Beliefs and Medical Practices of the Creek Indians." *Bureau of American Ethnology Annual Report* 42 (1928): 473–672.

Index

Agni, 1
Alabama Indians, 111–16
Alcor, 19
Aldebaran, 91
Anitsutsa — The Boys, 116, *see* Pleiades
Antares
  Coyote Star (Pawnee), 33
  Red Star (Pawnee), 47
Arapaho Indians, 65, 74
Artemis, 15
Assiniboin Indians, 63, 76
Australian Aborigines, 1

Bear, 33
Big Dipper, 15, 16, 18, 21, 25, 27, 81, 85, 89, 100, 111
  Celestial Canoe (Alabama), 111–13
  Ko'kinks (Klamath), 100
  Large Stretcher (Pawnee), 52
  Revolving Male (Navajo), 31
  Shield Stars (Cochiti), 38, 39
  Small Celestial Canoe (Alabama), 118
Big White Trail, *see* Milky Way
Blackfoot Indians, 63, 65, 68, 69, 74
Black Star, 47, 49, *see* Vega
Busk Ceremony, 113

Callisto, 15
Canopus
  South Star (Pawnee), 54
Capella
  Yellow Star (Pawnee), 47
Cassiopeia, 97
  Elkskin (Quileute), 106
  Revolving Female (Navajo), 31
Castor, 100
Cayuga Indians, 4
Celestial Canoe, 111–13, *see* Big Dipper
Chamberlain, Von Del, 47, 49, 54
Cherokee Indians, 3, 107–11, 116, 117
Cheyenne Indians, 63, 74
Chinook Wind Brothers, 106, *see* Orion
Choctaw Indians, 116
Chumash Indians, 79, 80, 82, 83, 85, 89, 90, 92, 93
Chunky, 116
Circle (or Council) of Chiefs, 47, 52, 60, *see* Corona Borealis
Cochiti Indians, 38, 40
Coeur d'Alene Indians, 20
Cold Wind's Canoe, 106, *see* Orion
Comanche Indians, 63
Corona Borealis, 18
  Circle of Chiefs (Pawnee), 47
  Old Camp (Arapaho), 78
Corvus
  Man With Feet Spread Apart (Navajo), 31
Council of Chiefs, 52
Coyote, 3, 7–9, 13, 22–24, 33, 34, 40, 82, 83, 91, 97, 100, 101
Coyote Star, 33, *see* Antares
Creek Indians, 111, 116
Crow Indians, 63
Cygnus, 93

Dakota Sioux Indians, 63, 73
Delphinus
  The Slingshot Stars (Cochiti), 38, 39
Dilyehe, 33–36, *see* Pleiades
Dove Maidens, 41–43

Earth Lodge, 47
Elkskin, 97, *see* Cassiopeia
Evening Star, 46, 59, *see* Venus
  Lone Star, 76

First Big One, 31, 35, *see* Scorpius
First Earth Lodge, 46
First People, 84
First Slender One, 35, *see* Orion
Fixed Star, 65, 69, *see* North Star

Gabrielino, 79, 80
Gatayu'sti, *see* chunky
Gemini
  Bow (Klamath), 100

Haida Indians, 96
Hard Flint Boys, 34, *see* Dilyehe, Pleiades
Hindus, 1
Hogan, 29, 30
Hopi Indians, 37
Horned Rattler (Navajo), 33
Hudson, Travis, 90
Hutash Ceremony, 85

Iroquois Indians, 107

Journey of the Piñon Gatherers, 93, *see* Milky Way

Kiowa Indians, 63, 65
Klamath Indians, 100
Ko'kinks, 100, *see* Big Dipper
Kwakiutl Indians, 96

Lambda and Upsilon Scorpii, 54
Large Stretcher, 52, *see* Big Dipper
Librado, Fernando, 89, 90
Little Dipper
  Little Stretcher, or Small Stretcher Bearing a Sick Child (Pawnee), 52
Little Stretcher, 52, *see* Little Dipper
Lone Star, 76, *see* Evening Star
Luiseno Indians, 83, 84, 91

Mandan Indians, 63
Man with Feet Spread Apart, 31, *see* Corvus
Mars, 45
Meteor, 49
Micmac Indians, 16, 18, 20
Milky Way, 24, 52, 76, 93, 117, 118
  Journey of the Piñon Gatherers (Chumash), 93
  Where the Dog Ran (Cherokee), 117–18
  Which Awaits the Dawn (Navajo), 33
Mohawk Indians, 4
Monache Indians, 9
Moon, 66–68
Morning Star, 40, 46, 47, 60–62, 65–68, 76, 83, *see* Mars

Navajo Indians, 28–31, 34–36, 38, 44, 55
North Fire, 31, *see* North Star
North Star (Polaris), 15, 16, 25, 52, 65, 69, 70, 81, 84, 85, 97, 111
  The Fixed Star (Blackfoot), 65
  North Fire (Navajo), 31
  Star That Does Not Walk Around (Pawnee), 52, 69, 70, 73
  Star That Never Moves (Chumash), 82, 83, 85

Old Camp, *see* Corona Borealis
Omaha Indians, 63, 70, 73
Oneida Indians, 4
Onondaga Indians, 4, 6
Oot-kwa-tah, 6, *see* Pleiades
Orion, 1, 37, 92, 93, 100, 106
  Chinook Wind Brothers (Wasco), 106
  First Slender One (Navajo), 35
  Three in a Row (Chumash), 92
  Young Men, 1

Pawnee Indians, 44, 45, 47, 52, 56, 62, 63, 73, *see* Skidi Band
Peon, 83
Picuris Indians, 41
Pitahawirata, 60
Pleiades, 1, 2, 3, 4, 9, 13, 14, 16, 37, 76, 89, 90–92, 100, 116
  Anitsutsa — The Boys (Cherokee), 116
  Dilyehe (Navajo), 31
  Eight Wise Men (Chumash), 89–90
  Hard Flint Boys (Navajo), 34
  Oot-kwa-tah (Onondaga), 6
  Seeds (Zuni), 2
  Seven Sisters (Luiseno), 91
  Seven Stars (Assiniboin), 76
  Seven Stars (Cochiti), 40
  Seven Stars (Pawnee), 55, 56, 58
Pleione, 1
Polaris, *see* North Star
Pollux, 100
Pot Rest Stars, 38–40
Pueblo Indians, 28, 37, 38

Quileute Indians, 97

Rabbit Tracks, 31, *see* Scorpius
Red Star, 47, *see* Antares
Revolving Female, 31, *see* Cassiopeia
Revolving Male, 31, 35, *see* Big Dipper

Sacred Pole, 73
Sacred Wheel, 76
Scorpius, 54
  First Big One (Navajo), 31, 35
  Rabbit Tracks (Navajo), 31
  Swimming Ducks (Pawnee), 54, 55

Seeds, 2, *see* Pleiades
Seneca Indians, 4
Seven Brothers, 76, *see* Pleiades
Seven Sisters, 91, *see* Pleiades
Seven Stars, 40, 55, 56, 58, 76, *see* Pleiades
Shasta Indians, 7
Shield Stars, 38, 39, *see* Big Dipper
Sirius, 1, 54, 55
  White Star (Pawnee), 47
Siva, 1
Skidi Pawnee, 44–47, 49, 52, 54–60
Sky Country, 58, 66, 68, 77, 78, 89, 110, 114, 115, 117
Slingshot Stars, 38, 39, *see* Delphinus
Small Celestial Canoe, 118, *see* Big Dipper
Small Stretcher Bearing a Sick Child, 52, *see* Little Dipper
Snohomish Indians, 25
South Star, 54, *see* Canopus
Star Picture Tipi, 65
Star That Does Not Walk Around, 52, 69, 70, 73, *see* North Star
Star That Never Moves, 82, 83, 85, *see* North Star
Stories
  Anitsutsa — The Boys, 116
  Baakil and His Five Wives, 13
  Basket Woman, Mother of the Stars, 58
  Black God and His Stars, 29
  Bright Shining Old Man, 4
  Celestial Bear, 16
  Celestial Canoe, 111
  Chinook Wind Wrestles Cold Wind, 102
  Coyote Loves a Star, 100
  Coyote Scatters the Stars, 40
  Door through the Sky, 109
  Dove Maidens, 41
  Eight Wise Men, 89
  Elk Hunters, 25
  Elkskin, 97
  Fixed Star, 65
  Grizzly Bear Brother-in-Law, 20
  How Coyote Arranged the Night Sky, 21
  How Rattlesnake Had His Revenge, 83
  Journey of the Piñon Gatherers, 93
  Land of the Dead, 80
  Little Girl Who Scatters the Stars, 37
  Raccoon's Children and Baby Coyote, 7
  Rolling Skull (The Seventh Star), 56
  Sacred Pole, 69
  Seven Boys-Turned-Geese, 85
  Seven Sisters, 91
  Seven Stars, 76
  Seventh Star, 56
  Sky Coyote, 82
  Sun Dance Wheel, 73
  What the Stars Are Like, 110
  Where the Dog Ran, 117
  White Elk, the Bear Man, 60
  Wild Onion Women, 9
  Wolf and the Crane, 92
Sun, 66, 68
Sun Dance, 74
Sun Dance Lodge, 75
Swimming Ducks, 54, 55, *see* Lambda and Upsilon Scorpii

Tachi Yokuts Indians, 13, 92
Tapirape Indians, 2
Taurus
  Young Men, 12
Three in a Row, 92, *see* Orion
Thunder, 33
Tipi, 65
Tlingit Indians, 96

Ursa Major, *see* Big Dipper
Ursa Minor, *see* Little Dipper

Vega, 49
  Black Star (Pawnee), 47
Venus, 45

Wasco Indians, 21, 104
Where the Dog Ran, 118, *see* Milky Way
Which Awaits the Dawn, 33, *see* Milky Way
White Star, 47, 54, *see* Sirius
Wishram Indians, 21

Yellow Star, 47, *see* Capella
Young Men, *see* Orion, Taurus

Zeus, 1, 15
Zuni Indians, 2, 37